shantung
black tiger

WEATHERHILL
NEW YORK
TOKYO

SHANTUNG BLACK TIGER

a shaolin fighting art of north china

TJOA KHEK KIONG
DONN F. DRAEGER
QUINTIN T. G. CHAMBERS

visual presentation: pascal krieger

First edition, 1976

Published by John Weatherhill, Inc., 149 Madison Avenue, New York, New York 10016, with editorial offices at 7-6-13 Roppongi, Minato-ku, Tokyo 106, Japan. Copyright © 1976 by John Weatherhill, Inc.; all rights reserved.

Library of Congress Cataloging in Publication Data: Tjoa, Khek Kiong. / Shantung Black Tiger : a Shaolin fighting art of north China. / 1. Hand-to-hand fighting, Oriental. / I. Draeger, Donn F., joint author. II. Chambers, Quintin, joint author. III. Title. / GV1112.T58 / 796.8'153 / 76-18800 / ISBN 0-8348-0122-1

contents

preface

THIS BOOK OFFERS an introduction to the fascinating subject of what some people, through disregard for its proper name, call "Chinese boxing" or "Chinese karate." The book does indeed deal with Chinese hand-to-hand tactics of a sparring and grappling nature, and each of the above terms has some merit when used to describe the fighting art presented here. But because there are proper Chinese names that describe the Chinese hand-to-hand systems, these native terms are preferred and will be used throughout this book; unless otherwise stated, all such terms will be given in their Mandarin form.

Chinese methods of sparring and grappling, both with and without weapons, are numerous. No complete survey has ever been made of these methods as systems, but were such a survey made it would reveal that these systems number more than one thousand. Though Chinese hand-to-hand systems are well known in Asia, they are relatively unknown in the Western world. Not all of these systems of sparring and grappling are genuine fighting arts, in spite of claims made to that distinction. For example, in Southeast Asia, where many hundreds of different hand-to-hand systems are actively practiced, some Chinese experts estimate that fewer than one dozen of the Chinese systems are truly fighting arts. A Chinese hand-to-hand system can have only one of the following primary purposes: (1) combat, (2) the promotion of health, or (3) theatrical performance. It is axiomatic that these totally different purposes cannot be combined in any way within one system if, at the same time, that system is to retain its optimum combative integrity of purpose.

8   No doubt because some systems of Chinese sparring and grappling adopted a more catholic attitude than others in regard to the dissemination of their teachings, it has become possible for a number of Westerners to learn something of those systems. Rarely, however, does the Westerner who practices them have the technical experience to enable him to judge whether or not what he practices is truly a fighting art. This book is therefore written specifically for the Westerner who is trying to learn more about the true Chinese fighting arts. The Shantung Black Tiger method of combat, described in English for the first time in this book, is little known outside China, where for many centuries the art was a closely guarded secret. Even today this art is rarely displayed, and, partly because of its seclusion, it retains its original purpose, that of being a genuine system of combat.

Because this book is the combined effort of a Chinese master-teacher of Chinese systems of hand-to-hand combat and two Westerners, something must be said of the division of responsibility for the authenticity of the contents. The technical aspects of the text and the photographs are the responsibility of the Chinese author, Tjoa Khek Kiong (also known as Leo Budiman Prakarsa because he is now an Indonesian citizen); the correct exposition in English of these technical matters has been the task of the Western coauthors. The photographs were taken by Donn F. Draeger.

The technical content of this book has been greatly simplified by reducing the use of complicated Chinese terms to a minimum, replacing them wherever possible with appropriate English terms that are not always intended to be literal translations. Yet some Chinese words have been retained, for they best describe the spirit and actions peculiar to the Shantung Black Tiger fighting art. A short glossary at the back of the book lists technical terms in the Mandarin dialect and gives their approximate English equivalents.

Abstract philosophical speculations, which are sometimes attached to Chinese hand-to-hand systems and are said to express the essence of all such systems, have been eliminated. Such speculations play no significant role in making the Black Tiger art more effective in combat; they are the products of scholars who were remote from the reality of combat, and are rarely considered by the actual exponents of this art. From the practical point of view, philosophy is useless. Legend and history, all too often equated by those who engage in the study and practice of the Chinese hand-to-hand arts, have also been eliminated, the authors preferring to get to the meat of the matter, that is, the how and why of the Shantung Black Tiger fighting art.

In revealing for the first time the tactics of the Black Tiger method of combat, the Chinese author hopes both to commemorate the greatness of the masters who developed this art in the past and to preserve the purity of the art for future generations. The two Western coauthors consider themselves fortunate to have had the opportunity to study something of the Black Tiger fighting art and to aid in its authoritative presentation.

The authors are extremely grateful to Tjoa Tjong Hian (Darmawan Prakarsa) and Tjoa Tjong Soan (Jany Tiara Prakarsa) for their unselfish cooperation in posing for the photographs that illustrate the practical applications of the Black Tiger fighting art. Special thanks are also due to Tjioe Tian Chong for the use of his private estate at Puntjak, West Java, where most of the photography was done; to Tan Koie Nio (Lily Rahmat), Lie Bun Pin (Benjamin Ramli), Lo Siauw Tjun, Djoko, Stephen Hua, and Dr. Ong Swee Chee for their aid in the tedious work of translating the Chinese terms; to Tan Goan Hoat (Tatang H.) for reading the manuscript and for his helpful suggestions for increasing its accuracy; and to Pascal Krieger for his original and creative book design and photographic layout, as well as for the excellent line drawings.

Tjoa Khek Kiong
Donn F. Draeger
Quintin T. G. Chambers

NOTE ON THE PHOTOGRAPHIC LAYOUT   In the action groups, classical and modern applications, and other photographic sequences of Black Tiger techniques, the order of the photographs always follows as closely as possible the actual direction of the exponent's movement. For this reason some sequences of photographs may begin on the right rather than the left or at the bottom rather than the top of a page. The beginning of each sequence is clearly indicated by a marker, and black arrows show the order in which to view the pictures. In the case of sequences that cannot be contained on two facing pages but continue overleaf, this is indicated by two large white arrows at the end of the first part of the sequence. In addition, the movement in the last photograph on that page is repeated in the form of a sketch so that the continuity of movement is maintained.

1   background

TERMS AND DEFINITIONS   An important aspect of Chinese culture, and one that has its roots in the prehistoric past, is the development of classical systems of sparring and grappling. The diversity of these systems is astonishing. Frequently, however, there is considerable confusion about their nature because of the great variety of terms that are used to identify and to describe them; different Chinese dialects use different terms to describe similar systems. Another reason for the confusion is the fact that some of these systems are intended to be used only for combat, others primarily for the promotion of health, and still others largely for theatrical performances. It is helpful, therefore, to begin any serious study of Chinese hand-to-hand systems with a short survey of Chinese martial terminology.

Wu-kung is a Mandarin expression that denotes any and all types of martial endeavor performed in a skillful and dedicated manner. This term refers to the effective use of force in martial matters; it is less applicable to efforts used for the promotion of health or those made in theatrical performance. Wu-kung thus encompasses the techniques and tactics of the fighting arts, as well as the martial ardor of the exponents who engage in them. *Wu-shu,* another Mandarin expression, literally means "martial art" or "martial arts." This term is used to describe all Chinese fighting arts collectively, including both weapon and weaponless systems, but it does not refer specifically to the martial ardor of the people engaged in them. Wu-shu thus has a more general meaning than wu-kung.

Two other Mandarin expressions are popular among the adepts of Chinese hand-to-hand systems. These are *ch'uan-shu* and *ch'uan-fa,* both of which imply "artful use of the fist or fists." These two terms are best used to describe unarmed tactics. Originally these terms were intended to refer to fighting arts, but in more modern times ch'uan-shu and ch'uan-fa have come to signify all manner of sparring, both Chinese and non-Chinese, and thus include systems used for combat, sport, the promotion of health, and theatrical performance. The expression *chung-kuo ch'uan,* meaning "Chinese fist-art," is more specific. Another Mandarin expression, *kuo-shu,* which means "national art," is also used to denote all Chinese methods of hand-to-hand tactics, no matter what their purpose.

Another term that describes Chinese hand-to-hand systems is the word *kun-tao.* This word belongs to the Hokkien dialect. It is a generic term that, like wu-shu, encompasses the study and practice of both empty-hand and weapon tactics, but expresses little of the martial spirit behind them. The ideogram for *kun* (also spelled *koon*) means "fist," and that for *tao* (also spelled *tow* or *tau*) means "head"; thus kun-tao means "the head of the fist." This definition, however, does not indicate the broad scope of kun-tao methods. Furthermore, it is not accurate to use the term to describe only empty-hand methods of fighting, since a substantial portion of kun-tao techniques makes use of parts of the body other than the fist. Nevertheless, the term is a popular one, being in common use among the hundreds of millions of Chinese and Malay people in Southeast Asia. In fact, in Southeast Asia the expression kun-tao is more commonly used than wu-shu, ch'uan-shu, or ch'uan-fa, which are terms preferred by the people of northern China.

Today the Cantonese expression *kung-fu* is much in use. But kung-fu refers only to the effort a person makes when he devotes himself seriously to some task. Whether or not the effort produces physical action is immaterial, so long as that effort is a dedicated one made in a serious frame of mind. A certain degree of skill is also inherent in the meaning of kung-fu. Thus, a person who paints his house, tends his garden, or does other domestic chores, or who applies himself assiduously to his trade or profession, is said to exhibit kung-fu. Kung-fu also connotes a creative spirit, as in the kind of effort made by an artist who sketches or paints, or by an artisan who molds ceramics or works with metal, wood, or other materials and produces skilled work of any kind. Kung-fu is definitely not a system of self-defense, nor any fighting art per se. It is not even proper to use the term kung-fu to describe the strenuous effort that must be made in training in or applying a fighting art: in this case, only the expression wu-kung is appropriate. But when an effort is made not specifically in connection with fighting arts, then it is proper to describe that effort as an example of kung-fu. For this reason the expression kung-fu may be correctly applied in connection with training in Chinese hand-to-hand systems whose purpose is sport, the promotion of health, or theatrical performance.

Chinese fighting arts were traditionally intended to be secret teachings, and *pai* were created to ensure the secrecy of all martial endeavor. A pai is an organization founded by a master of combat for the purpose of developing and perpetuating a specific style of a fighting art. In a broad sense, a pai is equivalent to a sect or a tradition.

Only people directly associated with a pai are eligible to receive the teachings of the master of that pai. Elaborate security measures are taken to avoid the betrayal of the techniques of the pai. Some pai are especially strict in matters of membership, restricting the choice of candidates for admission to the members of a particular family. Other pai are more liberal in their policies; they select freely from among those who are considered worthy of their teachings. In the past, however, Chinese people of dissimilar ethnic stock were not permitted to be members of the same pai. Non-Chinese in particular were forbidden even to see the genuine fighting arts, though outsiders might be permitted to witness those systems that stressed the promotion of health or that specialized in theatrical performance. Nevertheless, even a member of a pai may not receive the inner teachings of the master, that is, the most meaningful techniques of the pai, until he has undergone intense observation by the master over a long period; during this time the master evaluates the member in terms of ability, perseverance, and loyalty. Should the member fail to meet the criteria set by the master, though he may be retained as a member of the pai he will never be given its innermost secrets.

But time is a prying dimension against which the staunchest of traditions finds great difficulty in armoring itself, and some knowledge of fighting arts has been gained by Chinese people outside the pai that these arts were originally intended to serve. A limited number of non-Chinese people, too, have seen, if not studied, Chinese fighting arts. Even more non-Chinese people are today actively engaged in Chinese systems that stress sport or the promotion of health. However, the great majority of the genuine systems of combat are still unknown in the West.

Among the many hundreds of styles of Chinese hand-to-hand systems, two general types, based on geographical differentiations, can be identified. The styles that originate in North China and are most practiced by the people there may differ widely from the styles that were founded and are predominantly used by the people of the south. The northern Chinese are generally larger and physically more robust than their southern counterparts, conditioned by the more vigorous environment of the north. The people of South China tend to have a slighter build and therefore have accommodated their fighting styles to their own characteristic physique and mental disposition.

Northern combative styles are more acrobatic, dynamic, and forceful than those of the southern regions. North China is a mountainous area, and the people who live there naturally develop extremely long and strong legs. The people of the southern regions live mainly in fertile delta areas and, as agriculturists, make more use of their arms and hands than of their legs. Therefore fighting styles from the north depend on long-range actions in which the legs and feet are put to effective use. In the southern styles of combat, infighting tactics are preferred, and the exponents of these systems rely more on the clever use of their hands and arms. So accepted is this generalization that among the exponents of Chinese systems the saying "The leg of the north, the fist of the south" still applies when referring to the technique of an expert. The northern styles are also highly regarded for the skillful use made of the *chien,* a double-edged, straight-bladed long sword; the southern styles are respected for the expert use made of the *san-cha,* a three-pronged spear.

The manner of performing any Chinese fighting art is usually, though not always, associated with the fighting actions of animals. All ancient Chinese regarded what is beyond man's ability with tremendous awe. They developed great systems of thought based on the powers of nature. Included in their philosophies was a high regard for animals, who, though nonrational creatures, were nevertheless believed to be guided by the invincible forces of nature. The earliest Chinese fighting men paid particular attention to the ways in which animals fight, and devised methods of combat based entirely on such observations. The tiger (*hu*), the leopard (*pao*), the monkey (*hou*), the white crane (*pai-ho*), the snake (*she*), the bear (*hsiung*), the bull (*hsiung niu*), the eagle (*ying*), the ram (*yang*), and even the mythological dragon (*lung*) are beasts whose actions became the technical bases for various fighting systems. Similarly, an insect, the praying mantis (*t'ang-lang*), is the inspiration for other systems. The image of man serves in a similar capacity for a few extremely important systems, such as the Ta Mo (Bodhidharma), the *lohan* (*arhat,* or scholar-priest), and the *song-ti-chou* (emperor).

It is certain that the majority of the Chinese systems of sparring and grappling, regardless of their purpose, derive their inspiration, if not their actual techniques, from the fighting arts. The extant Chinese fighting arts continue in the tradition of their predecessors, for the most part without modification except for changes that make them more formidable in combat. But systems that have been created for the promotion of health or for theatrical performance must of necessity differ in many respects from fighting traditions if they are to realize their purposes. A brief examination of this important fact is essential for a fuller understanding of Chinese hand-to-hand systems.

Though some Chinese systems show a growing tendency to be conducted as competitive sports, their primary purpose remains either the promotion of health or theatrical performance. The genuine fighting arts, the wu-shu, are not sports. These systems cannot be contested in terms of championships, for to do so would be to expose the participants to serious danger, even death. Systems that permit sport competition are restricted by very strict rules that limit not only the scope of the techniques to be used but their applications as well, in order to provide the participants some margin of safety as they compete. Though sport competitions approximate combat more closely than do those systems that are exercised purely for health or theatrical performance, sport competition is not real combat. True combat has no rules, and therefore the only test of a fighting art must always remain the harsh reality of actual fighting.

Any benefit to health that may accrue to the trainee through the practice of a genuine fighting art is of secondary importance. The primary purpose of all training done in the wu-shu manner is to enable the exponent to wage effective hand-to-hand combat. Exponents of fighting arts, however, are concerned with toughening the mind and body, and therefore place emphasis on improving their health. Training methods that make the mind insensitive to adversity are considered worthwhile, and exercises that make the body more durable through physical exertion or better able to withstand an enemy are also assiduously practiced. Concentrated training in fighting arts (wu-kung) results in considerable physical damage to the trainee's body. Some of this damage is unavoidable, the natural result of traumas caused by the tremendous forces of physical contact. Still other physical damage is deliberately inflicted to promote a general toughening of mind and body. But the practice of fighting arts over an extended period of time involves the entire body in energetic exercise, and the health of any exponent will be improved. To become skillful in fighting arts requires an alert mind and a strong, flexible, and agile body, a combination that makes the exponent capable of taking instant action in an emergency.

The Chinese systems of sparring and grappling that are primarily performed in order to promote health are conducted in a way that will not overtax the trainee. These systems regard anything that tends to injure or strain the body as detrimental to their purpose, and religiously refrain from using the most drastic training methods of the fighting arts. Because their purpose is to promote health, training methods must be softened, and consequently the exponents so trained are not fully effective in combat. Any peripheral value, in terms of self-defense, that may be contained in the health systems is largely incidental and quite limited in scope.

background

18

The wu-shu are not performed theatrically, for the concept of entertaining an audience is completely alien to the exponents of true fighting arts. In order that the exponents may develop stronger bodies for combat, however, some systems place high value on the performance of acrobatic actions in the execution of techniques. Chinese systems whose purpose is to entertain an audience also require their exponents to make acrobatic actions. But there is an important difference between the acrobatics of the fighting arts and of the theatrical systems. Whereas the former employ acrobatic actions that are always made with combat situations in mind, the latter systems develop a gymnastic routine, which is actually choreographed, in order to gain the plaudits of an appreciative audience; their performances are almost always incompatible with the conditions of natural terrain that would be found in actual combat.

Masters of fighting arts sometimes differentiate the *nei-chia,* or "internal systems," and the *wai-chia,* the "external systems." The former are said to be based on *nei-kung,* or "inner strength," that is, on mental spirit (*i*), and rely more upon a "soft" or flexible approach to combat, yielding to force rather than opposing it. The latter systems are the "hard" methods, based more on physical toughness and the use of muscle for resisting actions through "outer strength," or *wai-kung.* Perhaps no Chinese system of sparring or grappling is either wholly soft or wholly hard in its methods, but those like *t'ai-chi ch'uan, pa-kua,* and *hsing-i* are traditionally said to be examples of the internal systems, while most Shaolin forms are regarded as external systems.

One of the most vigorous and powerful forms of Chinese combat is found in a Shaolin-derived system that was developed in North China. Known as the Shantung Black Tiger style, this system of fighting is centuries old—just how old is not known—and is extant. The Black Tiger system stems from a pai in Honan Province, but its teachings have been legitimately transmitted to some specially selected Chinese masters from South China. The Black Tiger fighting art combines the internal and external principles. The soft principles are characterized in this system by light, evasive actions, and stand in sharp contrast to the hard principles, which are heavier, more direct applications of force. When applying the soft principles, the exponent of the Black Tiger style seeks to avoid his enemy's focus of power, choosing rather to blend with it, misdirect it, and greatly reduce its intended effect. When applying the hard principles, the same exponent engages in harsh actions that intercept the power of the enemy, withstand it, and return an even more powerful force to subdue the assailant. Yet because of a tendency to favor the soft principles, the Black Tiger system is ideal for people of average physique and strength.

The Black Tiger system must always be practiced as *tao-chien,* that is, as a prearranged exercise. When performing the Black Tiger sequence of techniques you will be required to make certain maneuvers in a definite order and in a precise form that must never be changed. Do not underestimate the value of tao-chien, and do not regard this method as lacking combative realism. That the complete Black Tiger sequence shown in this book is based on hypothetical combat situations, conducted in a specific order and executed in a certain way, cannot be denied, but these situations are based on real-life combat. Tao-chien thus serves as a vehicle to commemorate combative events of the past. The modern exponent can share in centuries of fighting experience as preserved by the masters who developed the Black Tiger fighting art. The Black Tiger sequence of techniques, if correctly performed on a regular basis over an extended period of time, develops a functional fighting skill in the trainee. Beyond this, the sequence also provides the basis of a mental discipline from which the trainee can gain self-control and confidence in his ability to defend himself. When the trainee attains a high degree of skill in performing the entire sequence of Black Tiger techniques, he can easily detach any single movement or a short series of movements, or mix the individual movements out of order, and apply them automatically to whatever combative situation may arise.

ABOUT WEAPONS Those wu-shu that are realistic fighting arts do not require that the exponent be unarmed in combat. But because he may be forced to fight unarmed, a substantial portion of wu-shu training is devoted to the development of an effective way of waging unarmed combat. Yet the study of weapons (*kung-chi*) is also an important aspect of all genuine fighting arts.

Though a trainee begins his study of wu-shu by learning how to use major parts of his body—hand, arm, elbow, knee, foot—as weapons, once the rudiments of this kind of training have been learned the trainee is required to undergo extensive study of the use of implemental weapons. The classical systems of Chinese fighting arts possess a unique feature in this respect. The movements that a trainee makes when executing a technique while unarmed can be repeated in exactly the same way when he is armed without danger to himself. This fact indicates the creative genius of

20   the masters who designed the classical systems of combat. It also ensures that no skills learned are wasted.

A great variety of weapons is used in the wu-shu. The exponent is expected to become skilled in the use of both weapons and ordinary tools and other articles used in daily life. Some of these instruments are common to all styles of wu-shu, while others are the particular or special weapons only of certain styles.

Some of the commonest weapons used by the exponents of wu-shu are the following: *chien*, a straight, double-edged long sword; *tao*, a curved, single-edged long sword; *ch'iang*, a straight-bladed spear; *san-cha*, a three-pronged spear, or trident; *kwan-tao*, a long-handled halberd; *swang-so-tai*,

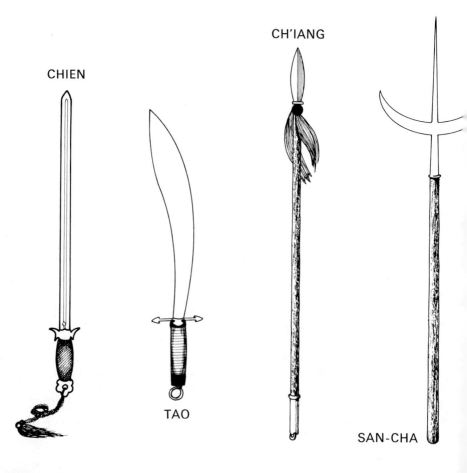

CH'IANG

CHIEN

TAO

SAN-CHA

a short-handled halberd; *kung-pang,* a staff; *cha,* a two-tined iron trun-cheon; *san-chet-kwon,* a three-sectioned stick; and *piao,* a short throwing blade. (The drawings below are not to scale.)

Among the many articles of everyday use, the following are most com-monly employed as weapons by exponents of Chinese hand-to-hand sys-tems: rakes, hoes, benches, umbrellas, walking sticks, and baskets of vari-ous types. Indeed, there is no rule limiting the articles that may be used. Thus it can be said that no well-trained exponent of Chinese fighting arts, though he be unarmed, is ever without a weapon. When an emergency arises, he can instantly arm himself by selecting something from among the many objects that surround him in daily life.

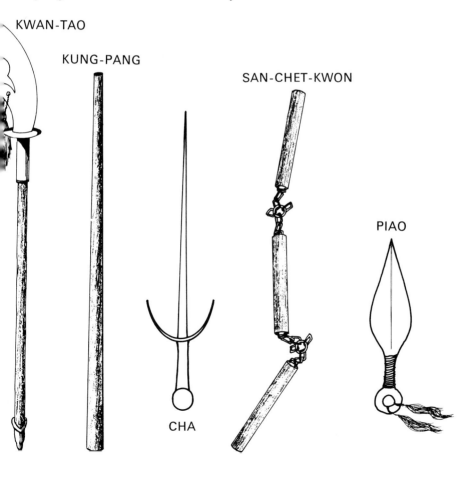

KWAN-TAO

KUNG-PANG

SAN-CHET-KWON

PIAO

CHA

background

2

the elements
of training

THERE ARE SIX FUNDAMENTAL special characteristics of the Shantung
Black Tiger fighting art that must be thoroughly understood by each
trainee as he initiates and continues his study of this art: (1) the theory
of multiple enemies, (2) forming the fist, (3) other anatomical weapons, (4)
the stances and postures, (5) preparation for movement, and (6) hand actions, blows, and kicks.

THE THEORY OF MULTIPLE ENEMIES   In the execution of the techniques of the Black Tiger art, you must always assume that you are sur-
rounded by a number of enemies who are trying to take your life. At times
you deal with only one enemy at a time; at other times you deal with two
enemies simultaneously. Your actions must always be made in the appropriate directions to meet, neutralize, and subdue all threats to your person.

FORMING THE FIST   The particular pai in Honan province from which
the Black Tiger fighting art derives employs a fist (*ch'uan*) made in a very
particular way; no other formation of the fist is used in this art. To make
this special fist:

THE BLACK TIGER FIST

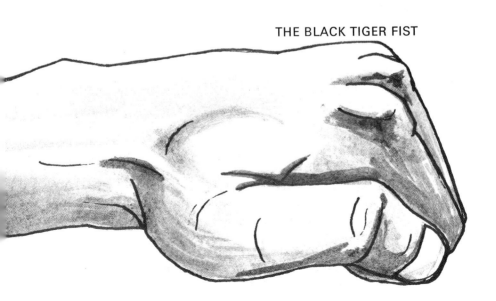

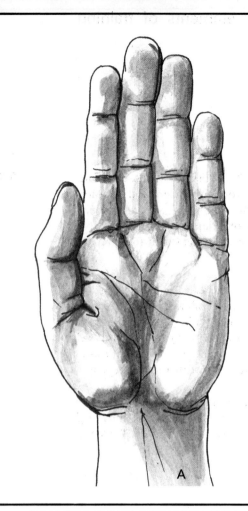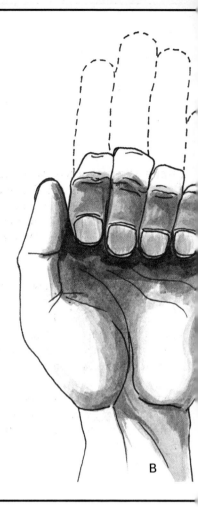

A   B

FORMING THE BLACK TIGER FIST

1. Open the hand and stretch the fingers, pressing them tightly together; place the thumb straight along the forefinger side of the hand (A).
2. Curl the fingers, tucking the fingertips into the palm as close as possible to the junction of the fingers with the palm (the base knuckles); keep the thumb in contact with the forefinger edge of the hand (B).
3. Clench the hand tightly so as to bury the fingertips deeply in the palm; the thumb allows the fingers to move (C).
4. Make a tight fist by bringing the inner side of the thumb down against the exposed side of the curled forefinger; press the thumb downward against this surface to lock all fingers in place (D).

Carefully study this manner of making the Shantung Black Tiger fist, and be certain that you can form this important anatomical weapon quickly. You will have occasion to make this fist, open it, and remake it many times over.

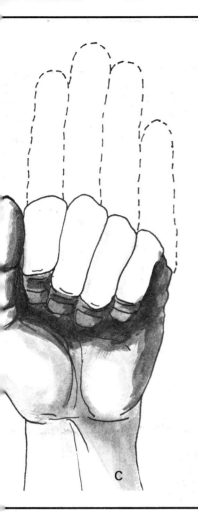

C

D

The fist formed in this way, because of the pressure of the thumb, is said to be stronger on impact than is a fist formed in the conventional manner with the thumb curled over the front of the fingers (E); the fingers of the Black Tiger fist are less liable to slip and thus decentralize the force of the blow.

E

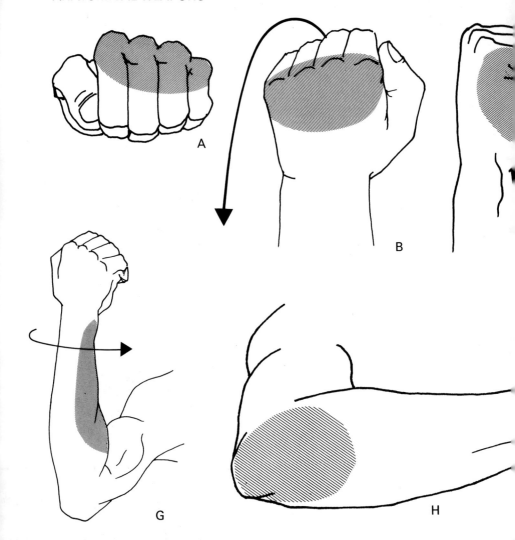

ANATOMICAL WEAPONS   The fist is a very important anatomical weapon for the exponent of the Black Tiger fighting art. It is primarily used in three ways:

1. as a fore-fist, a primary weapon (A);
2. as a back-fist, a primary weapon (B);
3. as a bottom-fist, a primary weapon (C).

The hand is also formed for secondary use:

4. as a beak-hand (D);
5. as an open palm (E), used flat or in conjunction with
6. the knife-edge of the hand (F).

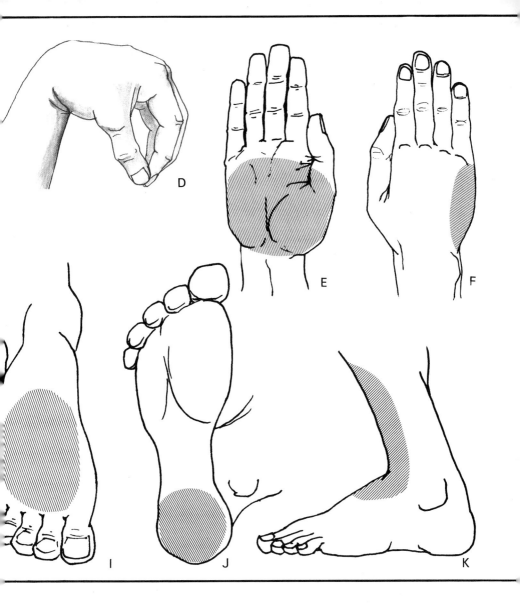

The arm, used as a weapon, makes use of the following:

  7. the outer forearm, a primary weapon (G);
  8. the elbow, a secondary weapon (H).

The feet and legs are always used as primary weapons. Striking surfaces include:

  7. the instep (I);
 10. the heel (J);
 11. the instep–lower shin area (K).

The specific uses of these natural weapons are discussed in chapter four.

30

STANCES AND POSTURES   Stance refers to the position of the feet and legs, posture to the position of the entire body. Thus it is possible for you to assume different postures, say an erect or a crouching posture, from the same stance. Eight combinations of stance and posture, called *sze,* are fundamental to the execution of the Black Tiger fighting art.

1. *Chi-ma-sze,* the "horse-riding" or deep crouching stance, is made with no change in stance as postures are taken on both the left and the right sides. First assume the basic horse-riding stance. Position the feet apart, toes pointing outward, at a distance that is at least twice the width of the shoulders. Sink down by bending the knees until the thighs are about parallel to the ground; center your weight evenly between both feet. Keep the upper body erect but make the back concave by pushing the buttocks

HORSE-RIDING STANCE

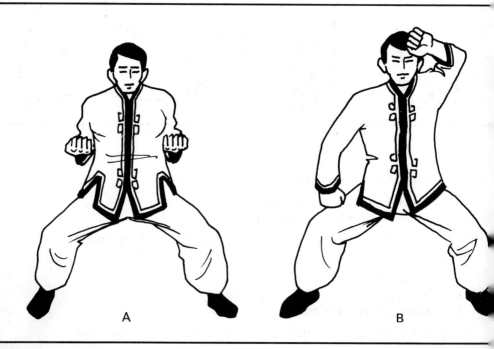

A   B

out to the rear. Position both arms, hands held as fists, knuckles down, so that the fists are at chest level just below the breastline, elbows bent and held well back, close to the body (A).

Assume a left posture while in the horse-riding stance by lowering your right arm, hand still clenched as a fist, and place that fist, knuckles forward, on the upper part of your right thigh close to the hip; raise the left arm, left hand also held in a fist, bending the elbow so that the fist is brought to a position in front of and a little above the center of the forehead, knuckles facing the rear (B).

Change to a right posture by simultaneously extending and lowering the left arm and raising the right arm to reverse their positions (B–D). Notice that with the change of arm positions the feet do not move, nor does the body rise and fall.

C   D

2. *Kai-tang-sze,* the "chest-opening" or lunge stance, is made with a similar symmetrical posture on both the left and the right sides. A shift in stance accommodates the change of posture from left to right.

Assume this stance, made first on the left, by lunging forward onto the left leg; bend the left knee enough that the shinbone of that leg is approximately at a right angle to the ground; stretch the right leg fully, keeping the right foot flat on the ground. Distribute your weight on a sixty-forty basis that favors your advanced left leg. Interlace the fingers of your hands, turning the thumbs downward as you extend both arms, palms forward, in the direction the left foot is pointing; lock the arms in a fully extended

LUNGE STANCE

D   C

position and stretch them forward and downward. Keep the upper body erect, chest up, chin in, and jut your buttocks out backward so that the back is concave (A).

Assume a right stance and the corresponding change of posture by raising both arms while fully extended, hands interlaced, in a big arc upward to your left-front corner, over and around behind your body; twist your body to your right. As your arms move across to the right of the vertical centerline of your body, pivot both feet in place to accommodate the further twist of your body just as you lower your arms and lunge forward onto your right leg (B–D). The body remains upright throughout the action.

B   A

3. *Tu-lie-sze,* the "one-leg" or balancing stance, is made with a similar symmetrical posture on both the left and the right sides. Actual linear displacement of the body and a change of direction accompany the change of posture from left to right.

Assume a left stance first. Stand fully balanced on the right leg, right foot flat on the ground. Raise the left leg, bent at the knee, and place the sole of the left foot on the right inner thigh just above the knee. Extend both arms, the right hand raised high overhead, palm open and facing the side, and the left arm brought well back to the left rear corner, hand held in a beak-hand (A).

BALANCING STANCE

A   B

Change to a right stance by leaping forward off the "platform" right leg to deliver a forward snap-kick with the left foot to groin level, using the instep as a striking surface. Leap as far as possible, turning 180 degrees to your right after you have kicked, to face the direction from which you have just come. As you leap and kick, land on your left foot, but change arm positions so that your left arm is raised and your right arm comes into a low position. Using your left leg as a platform leg, raise the right leg, bent at the knee, and place the sole of that foot on the left inner thigh just above the knee (B–D). The body does not face the direction of the leap but is slightly turned in a half-frontal posture with the raised-arm side forward.

C

D

A   B

READY STANCE

4. *Sien-chi-sze,* the "fighting cock with spurs" or ready stance, is made with a similar symmetrical posture on both the left and the right sides. Actual linear displacement of the body accompanies the change of posture from right to left.

Assume this stance first on the right side by shifting your weight well back over the rear left leg. Bend the left knee, toes pointing outward to the left front. "Float" the advanced right foot with only the toes, turned in, touching the ground; keep the knees well together to protect the groin. The distribution of body weight is approximately sixty-forty between the rear and forward legs, respectively. Bend your upper body slightly forward while making your back concave, buttocks jutting out to the rear. Extend both arms in front of the body, the right arm leading the left arm, both hands held in fists, knuckles down, with the left fist to the inside of and higher than the left elbow (A).

Change to a left stance by shifting your weight onto the advanced right foot, after pivoting the toes to the right and stepping the left foot forward ahead of the right foot, toes turned inward. Shift your weight over the rear right leg, bending that knee, and "float" the now advanced left foot (B). Notice that with the change of stance the body does not rise or fall but moves

EXERTION STANCE

E   D

forward at the same level; the body does not directly face the direction of movement but is slightly turned in a half-frontal posture facing the side of the retreated leg.

5. *Ten-san-sze,* the "mountain-climbing" or exertion stance, is made in the manner of a tiger as it ascends a steep mountain. A shift in stance accommodates the change of posture from the left to the right side.

Assume this stance first on the left by positioning the feet well apart, left leg advanced; center your weight evenly between your feet, and keep both knees slightly flexed. With the upper body erect, extend and raise both arms, slightly bent at the elbows. Twist your body fully to the left as you bring the left arm high, palm facing the left, to your left side and behind you. Position the right arm, palm open and facing forward, at shoulder level in front of you (A).

Change to a right stance by bending forward and turning to your right. Swing both arms, extended and slightly bent at the elbows, forward and downward in a big arc across the front of your body as you turn. As your body passes the vertical centerline, come erect and raise both arms upward in a big arc, pivoting both feet in place to the right. Twist your body fully to the right as you spread both arms, the left arm coming to shoulder level, palm facing forward in front of you, the right arm coming up high and well back behind you, palm facing the right (B–E). Notice that the body must be in a frontal posture while in this stance.

C   B   A

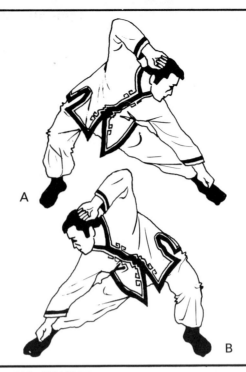

A

B

BOW-DRAWING STANCE

6. *Kai-kung-sze,* the "bow-drawing" or deep archer's stance, resembles the position an archer might take to shoot a target on a steep slope below him. It is made with a similar symmetrical posture on both the left and the right sides. A shift in stance accommodates the change of posture from left to right.

Assume this stance first on the left by positioning your feet very widely apart. Sink down into a low crouch, bringing your weight more over your bent right leg. Fully stretch the left leg but keep the left foot flat on the ground, toes pointing slightly inward. The distribution of body weight is approximately sixty-forty between the rear and advanced legs, respectively. Bend the upper body forward and down, facing the direction of your outstretched left leg. Extend the left arm, hand held in a fist with knuckles up, downward along the line of and to the inside of the left leg. Bring the right arm back, bending it at the elbow so that the right fist, knuckles facing the body, is positioned at the right temple (A).

Shift to a right stance and the corresponding change of posture by bending your left knee as you shift your weight onto the left leg; fully stretch the right leg. Change arm positions so that the right arm is extended, along the line of and to the inside of the right leg, hand held in a fist with knuckles up. Bring the left arm back, bending it at the elbow so that the left fist, knuckles facing the body, is positioned at the left temple. The relative distribution of body weight for the right stance is the same as for the left stance (B).

STEALTH STANCE

7. *Yeh-sing-sze,* the "walking and searching in the night" or stealth stance, resembles the movement of the tiger as it takes short, careful steps. This stance is somewhat similar to the ready stance but entails large swinging actions of the arms during linear movement, and is a deeper stance that uses a weight distribution of about seventy-thirty between the rear and advanced feet, respectively. It is made with similar symmetrical postures on both the left and the right sides. Actual linear displacement of the body accompanies the change of posture from left to right.

Assume this stance first on the left side by bending the right knee and shifting your weight well back over the rear right leg. "Float" the advanced left foot, toes in, with only the toes touching the ground, keeping the knee slightly bent as you do so; keep both knees well together to protect the groin. Position your upper body bent slightly forward; make your back concave by jutting your buttocks out to the rear. Extend the left arm, keeping it slightly bent at the elbow with the hand open and the palm facing forward at shoulder level. Bring your right arm well back behind you, pointing it downward, hand held in a beak-hand (A).

Change to a right stance by shifting your weight onto the advanced left leg, pivoting the toes of the left foot outward to the left, and stepping the right foot forward ahead of the left. Shift your weight over the rear left leg and "float" the advanced right foot, toes turned inward. Extend the right arm in front of you, keeping it bent at the elbow, palm open and facing inward; extend the left arm, hand held in a beak-hand, to the rear. Distribute your weight in the same way that you did in the left stance (B). Notice that the body does not directly face the direction of movement but is turned to a half-frontal posture that favors the side of the beak-hand.

8. *Kua-hu-sze,* the "tiger" or stalking stance, depicts the tiger in rhythmic movement as it quietly but powerfully stalks its prey preparatory to leaping. This stance is made with similar symmetrical postures on both the left and the right sides. Actual linear movement of the body occurs with the change of posture from left to right.

Assume this stance first on the left side by positioning your feet quite widely apart. Sink down, bending both knees, and shift your weight more onto the rear bent right leg. "Float" the advanced left foot, toes pointing inward at approximately a right angle to the rear right foot, toes just touching the ground. The distribution of body weight is approximately eighty-twenty between the rear and advanced feet, respectively. Keep the upper body erect, jutting your buttocks out to the rear to make your back concave. Raise both arms, keeping them slightly bent at the elbows. The left arm points forward, palm open and facing the front at face level; the right arm is brought high overhead to the right, palm facing outward (A).

TIGER STANCE

A   B

Change to a right stance by shifting your weight onto the advanced left leg, after pivoting the toes to the left, and centering your weight fully on the left leg; come into the erect position. Raise your right leg, bent at the knee, until the thigh is above the horizontal, with your foot fully flexed and your toes pointing downward. At the same time change arm positions, keeping both arms bent and both hands open, swinging the right arm forward, palm facing forward at face level; raise the left arm high overhead to the left, palm facing outward. Take a long step forward with the right leg, and as the right foot comes to the ground, "float" that foot at approximately right angles to the rear left foot, toes just touching the ground. Lower your body and shift your weight onto the rear left leg; the distribution of body weight is the same as in the left stance (B–D). Notice that the movement is characterized by the large action of the body as it bobs smoothly up and down.

C   D

PREPARATION FOR MOVEMENT   The exponent of the Black Tiger fighting art prepares to move forward from a fixed stance in a manner that he seldom varies whether he wishes to punch, strike, or kick the enemy. This method is best understood by describing the actual act of moving into a stance rather than the preparation required for making another forward movement. Through the remainder of this book, unless specifically stated otherwise, all forward movement (*pu-fa*) made in preparation for decisive actions of punching, striking, blocking, or kicking in the sequence of techniques dealt with in chapter four evolves from the "chest-opening" or lunge stance. The following provisions also apply:

1. When stepping forward, place your advancing foot on the ground, heel first, toes pointing inward; then step fully onto that foot (A).
2. When the advanced foot is stepped to the ground in the manner just described, that foot must be pivoted on the heel so that the toes face the new direction in which you intend to move *before* you take a step with the other, retreated foot (B, C).

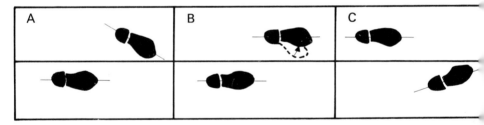

STEPPING MOVEMENT

HAND POSITIONS AND ACTIONS, BLOWS, AND KICKS   There are still other peculiarities in the positions of the hands and their actions, as well as in the manner of making blows and kicks, when executing the Black Tiger fighting techniques. The following points should be carefully studied.

Positions of the fists. You already know that the peculiar fist formation of the Black Tiger fighting art applies each time that a fist is made, regardless of its position in relation to the body. But when that fist is brought alongside the body preparatory to delivery of a punching action, the following points should be noted:

1. The arm must be bent, elbow well back, and the fist held, knuckles down, at chest level (A). **43**

2. A fist held in the above manner is closer to frontal target areas, such as the enemy's solar plexus and higher points of weakness, and thus the time for delivery of the punch is shorter than it would be for a blow delivered from the level of the hip.

The right fist, when positioned alongside the head at the right temple, is ready for blocking or striking actions. Observe the points listed below:

1. The fist must be held so that its undersurface is toward the enemy (B).
2. Incorrect positioning is shown in drawing C.

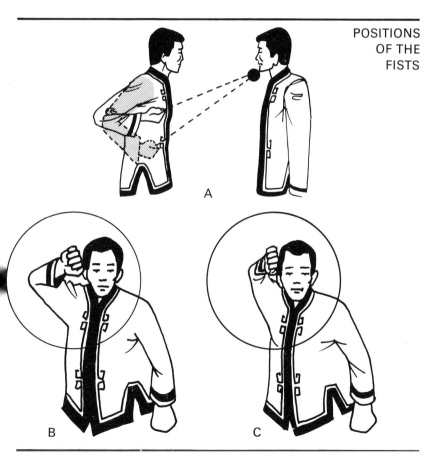

POSITIONS
OF THE
FISTS

A

B

C

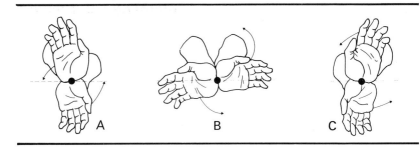

A   B   C

44

The lock-turning action. This action of the hands is called *fung-shou* because the hands move in unison as if working to turn a huge key in a lock. The action can be used effectively to block punches; when combined with the beak-hand it is also a parrying action that sweeps the attacking member aside. Perform the lock-turning action as follows:

1. Extend both arms in front of the body, palms open and facing each other, the right arm above the left arm.
2. Bring the heels of both hands together (A).
3. Keeping the heels of the hands together, rotate the hands clockwise until the left hand comes uppermost (B, C).

The hammer and the whip. Typical of the hand actions of the Black Tiger art are two back-fist blows, usually executed one after the other in rapid succession. The first, a devastating hammerlike action, is called *pung*. The ideogram for this term means "to knock down and cover the enemy's attack with the force of an avalanche." Indeed, this blow is used to smash down all that stands before one. The blow is usually aimed at the enemy's face or the top of his head. Perform the hammer blow with the left fist as follows:

1. Stand in the horse-riding stance, your left side facing the direction in which you wish to deliver the blow. Position both arms, bent at the elbow, in front of your body, hands in fists with knuckles down (A).

HAMMER BLOW

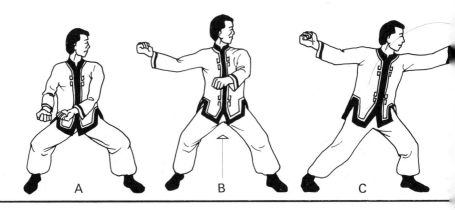

A   B   C

2. Begin to rise out of the crouch. Fold your left arm across the front of your body so that the fist, knuckles up, is to the rear. At the same time extend and raise your right arm, hand in a fist with knuckles down, to the rear (B).

3. Continue rising out of the crouch and bring the left back-fist over in a short arc (using the elbow as a pivot) in an overhead-downward trajectory to your left side. Shift into a left lunge stance as you focus the blow at head level; use the base knuckles of the first two fingers, not the back of the hand, as the striking surface. Raise your right arm, slightly bent and with fist held, knuckles down, high to the rear (C).

Pung, delivered with the left fist, is usually followed by *cha,* a whiplike action of the right fist. This too is a crushing blow. The ideogram for cha implies "to finalize an attack by chopping and pressing." Make this blow as follows:

1. Begin from the stance and posture in which you completed the hammer blow (A).

2. Twist your body to the left and swing your right back-fist forward in an overhead diagonal-downward trajectory to strike at the same target that you did with the hammer blow (the top of the enemy's head or his face). Use the base knuckles of the first two fingers as a striking surface. As you deliver this blow, withdraw your left fist, knuckles down, to a position alongside your body at chest level (B, C).

WHIP BLOW

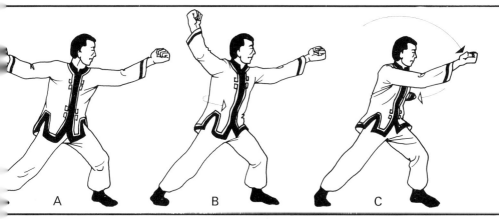

A   B   C

Do not confuse the delivery of the whip blow with the highly similar but different action in which the right outer forearm is used to block the enemy's attack. This blocking action is made in the following manner:

1. Stand in a left lunge stance and extend your left arm, hand held in a fist with knuckles up, fully in front of your body, as if just completing a thrust-punch with that fist. Position your right fist alongside your head at the right temple, undersurface of that fist toward the enemy (A).

2. Twist your body to the left and swing your right arm, well bent at the elbow, forward in a roundhouse diagonal-downward trajectory. Turn the fist in an outward direction as the arm moves forward. Begin to withdraw your left fist (B).

3. Focus the blow of your right outer forearm directly in front of your body with the fist at face level, knuckles toward the enemy. Withdraw your left fist, knuckles down, to a position alongside your body at chest level (C).

OUTER FOREARM BLOCK

The thrust-punch. This blow, called *kek,* is a straight-line punch made in a forward direction using either fist. It is delivered by the exponent as he stands in or is assuming a lunge stance. The fist being used starts from

LEFT THRUST-PUNCH

a position, knuckles down, alongside the body at chest level. Deliver the left thrust-punch as follows:

1. Stand in a left lunge stance and extend your right arm, slightly bent, in front of you at solar-plexus level; hold the right hand open, palm facing upward. Position your left fist, knuckles down, alongside your body at chest level (A).

2. Twist your body slightly to the left and raise the right hand, palm open and up, to the left front above face level (B).

3. Rotate the right arm counterclockwise to turn the palm downward and outward. At the same time withdraw the right arm until the clenched fist comes alongside the right temple, the undersurface of that fist facing the enemy. Twist your body to the right as you withdraw the right arm, and thrust the left fist straight forward in an extension of the vertical centerline of your body. Punch at shoulder level; screw the punch inward to bring the knuckles of the fist upward at the focus of the punch (C).

4. Use the base knuckles of the first two fingers as a striking surface.

5. You may seek any target on the enemy's vertical centerline, from the groin to between the eyes, though usually this punch is delivered to the chin or solar plexus.

48

Deliver the right thrust-punch in the following manner:

1. Stand in a left lunge stance as though you have just delivered a left thrust-punch; position your right fist, knuckles down, alongside your body at chest level (A).

2. Take a long step forward with your right foot, lifting that foot high in the air (B).

3. As the right foot comes to the ground in front of you, go immediately into a right lunge stance. At the same time thrust the right fist straight forward in an extension of the vertical centerline of your body. Begin withdrawing the left arm.

4. Punch at shoulder level; screw the punch inward to bring the knuckles of the fist upward at the focus of the punch. Bring the left fist, knuckles down, back alongside your body at chest level (C).

5. Use the base knuckles of the first two fingers as a striking surface.

6. Target areas on the enemy are the same as for the left thrust-punch.

RIGHT THRUST-PUNCH

The double thrust-punch. Both fists can be used simultaneously to deliver a double blow forward, to the sides, or forward and backward. When double thrust-punching forward:

ORWARD DOUBLE THRUST-PUNCH

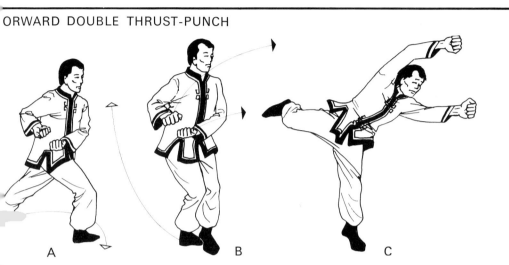

A   B   C

1. Assume a right lunge stance. Position both fists close together at the right side; hold the right fist, knuckles down, at chest level, and the left fist, also knuckles down, at the right hip (A).

2. Maintain the positions of the fists but shift your weight onto the right leg, the toes of the right foot turned inward to the left. Step the left foot forward into a position as close as possible in front of the right foot, turning the toes to the right (B).

3. Shift your weight onto your left leg, which is normally used as the platform leg for the double thrust-punch.

4. Bend forward from the hips and simultaneously punch with both fists as you stand fully on the left leg; the right leg must be thrust into the air to the rear, parallel to the ground, to act as a counterbalance. The trajectory of the thrust for each fist is circular: back, up, and over to the front. The right fist focuses at a position above the left fist, and both fists focus in a vertical position, that is, both palms face the right. With the focus of the double thrust-punch the body approximates the shape of the letter T (C).

5. Use the base knuckles of the first two fingers of each hand as the striking surfaces.

6. Aim the upper right fist at the enemy's face and the left fist at his solar plexus.

DOUBLE THRUST-PUNCH TO THE SIDES

When double thrust-punching sideways:

1. Stand in the horse-riding stance; position both fists at the sides, knuckles down, at chest level (A).
2. Simultaneously thrust both fists directly to the sides at shoulder level.
3. Screw each fist inward to bring the knuckles upward at the focus of the punch (B, C).
4. Use the base knuckles of the first two fingers of each hand as the striking surfaces.
5. You may seek any target on the centerline of the enemy, though usually this double thrust-punch is delivered to the solar plexus. Two enemies, one on each side of the exponent, can be dealt with in this fashion.

DOUBLE
THRUST-
PUNCH
TO FRONT
AND REAR

When using the double thrust-punch in a forward and backward direction:

1. Begin from the left ready stance (A).
2. Simultaneously thrust your advanced left fist forward and your right fist to the rear; punch at shoulder level.
3. Screw both punches inward to bring the knuckles of both fists upward at the focus of each blow (B, C).
4. Use the base knuckles of the first two fingers as striking surfaces.
5. Seek to strike forward at an enemy's chin, while at the same time striking backward at the face of another enemy behind you.

FORWARD BOTTOM-FIST PUNCH

The bottom-fist blows. The undersurface of the fist can be used as a durable striking surface when delivering powerful blows from a fixed lunge stance or during a shift in posture from one lunge stance to another. This kind of blow can be delivered against an enemy to either front or rear:

1. Stand in a right lunge stance, left arm fully extended to the front, as if completing a thrust-punch with the left fist. The right fist is held at the right temple, the undersurface of that fist facing front (A).
2. Pivot both feet in place to your left and shift your weight over the left leg to assume a left lunge stance. With this shift, swing your right fist forward in a circular trajectory that brings the knuckles down at chest level, and focus the blow in your new frontal direction. Use the palm of your left hand, fingers pointing upward, to support the striking right arm; place the left palm directly against the inside of the right arm at the elbow joint as the blow is focused (B, C).

3. Use the little-finger edge or bottom of the fist as a striking surface.

4. Seek any target on the enemy's lateral vertical centerline from head to ribs; the ribs are usually preferred.

To deliver the bottom-fist to the rear:

1. Stand in a left lunge stance, right arm extended forward, as if just completing a whip blow at head level. Your left fist is at your side, knuckles down, at chest level (A).

2. Twist your upper body to the right and deliver a forward thrust-punch at shoulder level with the left fist. At the same time withdraw the right arm by rotating the right fist, knuckles up. As the right fist comes alongside the right side of your head, strike to the rear by snapping the bottom-fist behind you (pivoting your arm on the elbow). Focus the blow, knuckles up, at head level (B, C).

3. Use the little-finger edge of the fist as a striking surface.

4. Seek any target on the enemy's body, but normally strike at the head.

REAR BOTTOM-FIST PUNCH

A   B   C

The forward snap-kick. The exponent of the Black Tiger fighting art sometimes uses the top of his right foot to deliver either a short or a long rising-arc kick as he is stepping forward with that foot. This kick, called *tie,* is especially effective when it is combined with, and masked by, a thrust-punch. Perform the forward snap-kick in the following manner:

1. Stand in the stance and posture in which you completed the right outer forearm block (A).
2. Shift your weight onto your advanced left leg.
3. Bend the knee of the retreated leg slightly and raise that leg, knee first, until the fully flexed foot, toes pointing downward, just clears the ground (B).
4. Kick forward by extending the lower leg, raising the thigh to do so; the trajectory of the kick is a rising arc to your front. As you kick, deliver a left forward thrust-punch; withdraw your right fist to a position alongside your body, knuckles down, at chest level (C).
5. Use the instep or the upper portion of the toes as a striking surface, and use the base knuckles of the first two fingers of the left hand as a striking surface.
6. Kick up under the enemy's groin or chin, and punch at his solar plexus or face.
7. Immediately after delivering the kick and thrust-punch, take a long step forward to the ground with the kicking right foot. At the same time deliver a right forward thrust-punch; bring the left fist alongside the body, knuckles down, at chest level (D).
8. Use the base knuckles of the first two fingers of the right hand as a striking surface.
9. Strike the enemy in the solar plexus or on the chin.

FORWARD SNAP-KICK

A   B   C   D

FORWARD THRUST-KICK

A   B   C

The forward thrust-kick. A powerful force is generated when a Black Tiger exponent chooses to use the heel of his left foot in either a short or a long rising-arc kick as he is stepping forward with that foot. Perform this thrust-kick as follows:

1. Stand erect, both feet together, your left side facing the direction in which you intend to kick. Stretch your left arm upward to the left, hand open and the palm facing away from you at a position above face level; bring your right fist, knuckles down, to your side at chest level (A).
2. Shift your weight onto your rear right leg. Maintain the relative positions of your arms and, without moving your right foot, kick your left foot, heel first, high into the air. Do this by twisting your body slightly to the left as you lift your left foot off the ground; bring your left thigh into a position parallel to the ground. Thrust your lower left leg, heel first, in a rising arc to the front; flex the toes upward toward the shinbone in order to jut the heel well forward (B).
3. Use the heel as a striking surface.
4. You may select any target on the enemy's body, but the solar plexus and the chin are the usual targets.
5. Immediately after kicking, take a long step forward onto the ground with the kicking foot and assume a left lunge stance; maintain your relative arm positions (C).

The whirlwind-kick. Typical of Black Tiger tactics is the *sien-fung-tie,* or "whirlwind-kick." This is a dynamic high roundhouse kicking action made with a whirling action of the body. Perform it in the following manner:

1. Assume a low posture by kneeling on the left knee; position that knee behind and outside the ankle bone of the right foot, and sit on the upraised heel of the left foot. Extend both arms, palms open, facing away from your body; the left arm inclines upward toward your left-front corner, while the right arm extends downward to the rear (A).

2. Come erect and shift your weight fully onto your advanced right leg. As you rise, maintain the relative positions of your arms (B).

3. Swing the left leg upward in a rising arc around and across the front of your body to the right, and allow the momentum thus generated to turn your body 180 degrees in that direction (C).

4. Use the instep or shinbone portion of the kicking leg as a striking surface.

5. The back, ribs, neck, and side of the enemy's head are the best targets.

6. Immediately after delivering the kick, take a step forward in the new direction with the kicking leg. Assume the tiger stance and posture (D).

WHIRLWIND-KICK

D   C   B   A

56

The low roundhouse-kick. This is a short-action kick called *chao-tie*. It is used to hook or reap the enemy's leg out from under him. Perform it as follows:

1. Take up a left bow-drawing stance but extend your left arm upward, hand open with the palm facing down, to your left-front corner; position your right fist at your side, knuckles down, at chest level (A).
2. Come erect and shift your weight fully onto your retreated right leg. Bring the left foot back to the platform foot, and at the same time sweep your left hand across your body to the right (B).
3. Leap off the right leg high into the air, turning in place 180 degrees to the left while in midair. Bring the left arm in to the body, palm down, at solar-plexus level, and raise the right arm, hand open, high overhead. While in midair, after turning left, hook-kick with the right foot at knee level (C).
4. Use the instep-shin portion of the kicking foot as a striking surface.
5. Aim the kick at the back of the enemy's advanced leg, as if to hook or reap him off that leg.
6. Drop down into a right bow-drawing stance. Your left arm remains folded across your body as your right arm, hand reclenched in a fist, beats downward and is focused, knuckles down, at knee level (D).

LOW ROUNDHOUSE-KICK

A　　　B　　　C　　　D

FORWARD DOUBLE SNAP-KICK

The forward double snap-kick. This acrobatic kicking technique is perhaps the most typical Shantung leg tactic. Called *liang-ke-tie,* it is executed while one is in midair, and is said to resemble the action of a fighting cock as it leaps forward onto its victim, clawing with its talons. Execute this double snap-kick in the following manner:

1. Stand in a left bow-drawing stance but assume a more upright posture. Position your right fist at the right temple, as required for the normal posture, but bring your left arm, hand open and palm downward, down in front of your body (A).
2. Leap off the retreated right leg toward the left, in the direction of the outstretched left leg. As you leap, turn your body to face directly forward in the direction of the leap. Deliver a short forward snap-kick with your left foot, and quickly follow it with a longer and more forceful snap-kick made with your trailing right leg; both kicks must be made while you are airborne (B, C).
3. The mechanics of and the striking surfaces and target areas for the forward double snap-kick are the same as for the single forward snap-kick. On landing, assume a right lunge stance and execute a right forward thrust-punch (D).

3 how to train

USE OF THE STANCES AND POSTURES   Expert skill in the performance of the Black Tiger fighting art can be achieved only when the trainee has a strong, flexible body that is capable of making quick, forceful movements over a long period of time without undue fatigue. Therefore a trainee should begin his training with strict attention to the first of all fundamentals: stance and posture. He is advised to make daily use of the eight different stances and postures in the traditional, time-proven way. Such training will greatly strengthen his body and will increase its stamina and thus its capacity for the strenuous exertion required in the performance of the Black Tiger art.

It is not necessary to do special warming-up exercises of a calisthenic nature when training in the style of the Black Tiger. Instead, the trainee should open each training session with a run-through of the stances and postures made in the traditional manner, as follows:

1. Assume each stance and posture consecutively, until all eight different positions have been taken.
2. Maintain each stance and posture without motion for at least one minute before going on to the next; as you develop more strength and stamina, the time limit may be extended to three minutes for each stance and posture.
3. Remember that each of the eight major stances and postures is made on both the left and the right side, except for the first one, the horse-riding stance, which consists of only one stance but has three postures. Thus, altogether, you will assume and hold yourself motionless in seventeen different positions for a total of at least as many minutes.

When you perform the actual sequence of techniques of the Black Tiger as described in chapter four, you may become aware of certain deficiencies in your stances and postures. Such defects as shaky stances, lack of balance, inability to assume low postures, or lack of power when you move from one stance to another are evidence more of muscular weakness than of lack of technical skill. If you detect any such deficiencies, the most effective corrective action you can take is to supplement your actual practice of the Black Tiger sequence with the traditional manner of using the eight major stances and postures just described. Concentrate on the stance and posture that gives you the most trouble, doubling the time that you hold yourself motionless in that position.

THE KEYPOINTS OF TRAINING   As you practice the Black Tiger sequence of techniques, pay attention to the following aspects of your performance: the order of the techniques, the correct form of the techniques, the rhythm of movement, strength climaxes, and targets.

Order of the techniques. The number of techniques in the sequence is fixed. The techniques are arranged in a logical order for the development of fighting efficiency. Make no change in this order of techniques. Practice as much of the entire sequence as you can; each time you train, practice what you know as a whole.

Correct form of the techniques. Through adherence to the details of correct form you will build efficient movement, which in turn lays the foundation for the development of speed and power, and thus of efficiency in combat. Follow carefully the descriptions of the illustrations in chapter four.

Rhythm of movement. The name of this fighting art suggests that the rhythm of your movement must emulate that of a tiger as it stalks its victim (closing with the enemy), leaps at and strikes its victim (contact with the enemy), and then withdraws (breaking contact with the enemy) in order to gather new strength for more action against the victim (enemy) should it be necessary. No description or illustration can explain this peculiar rhythm of movement; it must be experienced through intensive training.

Strength climaxes. Strength climaxes are those instants when your whole body is optimally focused in a critical action, as is necessary when you deliver a blow or kick against a chosen target area, that is, against an anatomical point on the enemy's body that, when struck, will disable him. But movement that takes you out of range of the enemy's counterattack can also be considered a strength climax. Learn to differentiate between these critical actions and those which you must make as preparation for closing with the enemy, actions in which you have yet to release your fullest concentration of force. Also recognize that a blocking or parrying action, for example, need not necessarily be a strength climax but may be simply preparatory to more forceful actions that will immediately follow. Recognizing strength climaxes lets the trainee use his energy economically.

Targets. The anatomical weaknesses of man's body are numerous, but the Black Tiger fighting art concentrates on relatively few of these weak points. Most of the vital points of the human body, and the most vulnerable ones, are in the so-called vertical centerline area. These weak points fall within the area formed by an imaginary band looped around the body from the top of the head to the base of the groin and back up to the head; the width of this imaginary band is about the same as the width of the head. Study the target areas suggested for each blow or kick in the sequence of techniques described in chapter four, and apply them as suggested.

DEVELOPING AND USING CH'I   The Chinese word *ch'i* has many different meanings, none of which, translated into English, truly conveys the essence of this amazing and important element of hand-to-hand combat. *Ch'i-kung,* or the power of ch'i, is demonstrable to a certain degree by those who genuinely possess it, but not all that people connected with the Chinese hand-to-hand systems claim to be ch'i is the genuine article. Many demonstrations that purport to show how ch'i works are in fact more akin to circus acts than to the fighting arts.

Those who seek to elevate ch'i to something mysterious or supernatural do a great disservice to the Chinese hand-to-hand arts. Instead, their efforts should be directed to pointing out the simple fact that ch'i is latent in everyone, and that it can be developed and released through rigorous training. The power of ch'i is indeed astonishing, but the development of ch'i comes only with long training and rigid discipline under the guidance of a qualified master.

You should think of ch'i as a kind of vital or nervous energy that is directed by the will. Ch'i is associated with the circulation of the blood, the breath, and the mind. But for the purposes of this book it is well to take the advice of Chinese masters of wu-shu, who discourage too much speculation about ch'i, especially the tendency of the novice to philosophize about it. Their simple advice is sound: "Don't ask questions, just practice, and you not only will develop ch'i but will come to understand it."

It is correct breathing that releases ch'i and constitutes the real source of your fighting power. Breathing is intimately connected with stance and posture, and helps the trainee to root himself to the ground. A simple procedure will enable you to breathe properly and will make possible the flow of ch'i and its concentration below the navel:

1. Inhale deeply but quietly through your nose.

2. Expand your abdomen as you inhale, as though trying to burst your belt; under no circumstances should you allow your chest to rise as you inhale.

3. Exhale forcefully, steadily, and quietly through your nose.

4. Contract your abdomen as you exhale so that this area shrinks in size.

Combine this manner of breathing with your daily use of the eight major stances and postures. As you stand motionless in each stance and posture, breathe in the manner just described. In this way you will greatly facilitate your development of nei-kung, internal strength, and its union with wai-kung, external strength.

Breathing is also directly connected with the application of strength climaxes. Only one rule applies in this connection: the instant you require the maximum use of focused body power (a strength climax), exhale. To inhale when applying a strength climax is a sure way of seriously weakening your ability to focus body power. Figures 1 through 17 on pages 66–67 show the opening movements of the sequence of techniques of the Black Tiger fighting art. They should be studied with care. In these movements is the basis for learning the method of correct breathing for the Black Tiger fighting art.

The actions shown in these illustrations, when performed with the breathing rhythm suggested, will promote the flow of ch'i during movement. Practice of just this small portion of the Black Tiger fighting art sequence will bring a multitude of benefits to the trainee in terms of learning how to make his body act in concert with his breathing. Stance, posture, stepping, the feeling of having a rooted foothold, the formation and reformation of the peculiar Shantung Black Tiger fist, weight distribution, the tigerlike rhythm of movement, and the application of the strength climax are all contained in this opening phase of the Black Tiger fighting art. But only when the entire sequence of techniques can be correctly performed will the trainee have established a considerable degree of both nei-kung and wai-kung.

Begin all movements in the sequence of techniques slowly. Try to maintain an even rhythm as you learn the mechanical transitions from one stance and posture to another. Once you are able to remember all the transitions and can perform the elements of correct form in each technique,

then you may go on and add the tigerlike pounce-and-retreat rhythm that
characterizes this fighting art.

You will soon discover through practice that stance and posture are even
more important than you had at first imagined. They are the very founda-
tions of fluency of movement, as well of accurate and effective delivery of
blows and kicks. Unless you learn to stand properly, that is, to gain the
correct foothold, you cannot hope to use your body as a unit and you will
never become very skillful. Study the various stances, and when you practice them, do so in connection with proper breathing. Develop the feeling·
of rooting your feet or foot to the ground. Accomplish this by holding
your strength downward, as though you were thrusting the legs or leg on
which you stand into the ground. Also pay close attention to the distribution of body weight in each of these stances and postures. Learn the way
of retreating and advancing, rising and sinking, to the required postures.
Give special attention to the subtle lateral movements made by stepping
one foot in front of or behind the other.

1. From the position shown in figure 1, slowly exhale
exhalation must be completed by the time you reach the
position shown in figure 4.

2. During the transition from the position shown in
figure 4 to the positions in figures 5 through 7, you must
inhale; reach full inhalation at the position shown in
figure. 7.

3. Exhale as you perform the action shown in figures
to 10.

4. Inhale once again as you make the movements illustrated in figures 10 to 14.

5. Finally, exhale as you do what is shown in figures
15 to 17.

reathing xercise

how to train

SOLO AND PARTNER TRAINING   To train alone is called *lien tao-chien*. Your initial practice of the Black Tiger art must be made in this manner. When you can perform the entire sequence of techniques with confidence, as evidenced by a continuous and smooth flow of movement from one technique to another, you may then test your abilities against a training partner.

Training with a partner is called *twee-chee tao-chien*. Use the combative situations described in chapter five for this kind of training. But before you do so, make sure that your training partner is also trained in the solo method of the Black Tiger fighting art. Working with a trained partner not only will ensure that you learn the techniques more easily but will bring a measure of safety to your training that is unattainable when one or both trainees are inexperienced. The actions required of the trainees in the self-defense applications are rapid; if improperly performed, they can result in serious injury to one or both training partners.

The combative situations and responses described and illustrated in chapter five are most effectively learned when both training partners assume their respective roles of attacker and defender a number of times consecutively before exchanging roles. In this way, through the drill or repetitive method, the mechanical actions that are required of the trainees in each situation will be quickly learned and reinforced and the trainees' technical skills greatly improved.

TOUGHENING YOUR ANATOMICAL WEAPONS   It has already been pointed out that the Black Tiger art makes use of both internal and external principles. This fighting art is thus a blend of the so-called soft and hard principles of combat, essentially a unity between actions that are nonresistant or pliable and those that are resistant, stiff, and harshly made.

Harsh actions, in which parts of the body are used as weapons to deliver blows and kicks, require that the part of the anatomy being used be able to sustain the great force that is generated when it is used as a striking surface against a target area on the enemy's body. In relation to these harsh actions, however, it must be pointed out that the use of hands and arms as weapons predominates over that of the legs and feet. Traditionally, some kind of footgear is always worn by the exponent of the Black Tiger fighting art, therefore his feet are to some degree protected from injury that might be caused by kicking. The hands and arms, being unprotected, are more exposed to injury.

In spite of the chance of injury to the hands and arms, no special training method for toughening them need be practiced by the trainee. Such training is optional. The smashing of pieces of wood, tile, or stone and similar practices for toughening the hands and arms are scrupulously avoided by the Black Tiger specialist. This is because the techniques of his art are based on scientific principles of human anatomy and physiology. These techniques specifically require that all blows be delivered against the enemy's vital areas, that is, against the weakest points on his body. Rather than blunder wildly into hard and resistant areas, which may produce injury to the striker's hands and arms, the exponent of the Black Tiger art selects only those targets that can be effectively struck with the hand and arm in their normal state of development.

As the trainee gains experience in the Black Tiger art, however, he may wish to improve the natural durability of his hands and arms. He can do this by carefully beating his hands and arms on such objects as sandbags, blocks of wood, and stone, striking at them with controlled force and in the manner prescribed by the actual techniques of the Black Tiger art. He can even strike arm against arm and fist against fist with a training partner, as shown on page 70. Whatever the method used for toughening his anatomical weapons, the trainee should ensure that it is a sensible one; it must not inflict damage that will deform and disable him.

TOUGHENING ANATOMICAL WEAPONS: HANDS AND FEET

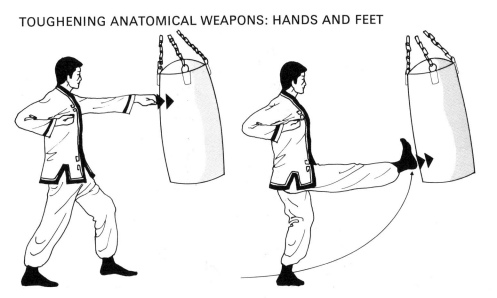

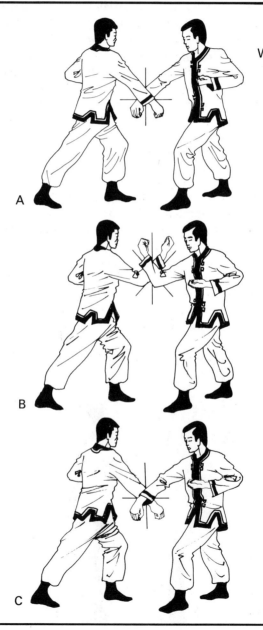

TOUGHENING
ANATOMICAL
WEAPONS: ARMS

A

B

C

It is a time-honored custom for all exponents of Chinese hand-to-hand systems, regardless of the purpose of the systems, to use special medicines after every training session. The composition of these medicines varies with each master-teacher who concocts them and directs their use; all formulae for these medicines are considered secret, to be divulged only to those trainees whom the master most trusts and respects.

THE HAND-SIGN OF THE BLACK TIGER PAI   All Chinese hand-to-hand systems, regardless of their purpose, make use of certain hand-signs or gestures. Each pai has its own special hand-sign, which is recognized as being the sign and countersign of that pai. The hand-sign symbolizes many different concepts, some of which include complex religious or political significance. Only the members of a pai understand the full meaning of the hand-sign of their pai, for it is kept secret.

The hand-sign of the Black Tiger pai is made by bringing the open left hand, palm downward, over the clenched right fist, holding the arms bent and parallel to the ground in front of the body at chest level, as shown in the drawing. Each and every exponent of the Black Tiger fighting art

makes use of this hand-sign at specific times to illustrate various meanings inherent in the spirit of the pai. The following meanings can be revealed:

1. A sign of respect from the exponent making it to the founder and past masters of the art, to all those who have practiced the art, to all those who currently practice the art, to those who watch his performance, and to Chinese wu-shu in general.

2. A philosophical symbol: the open hand represents *yin,* the passive, negative, "female" principle of the universe; the clenched fist represents *yang,* the active, positive, "male" principle. These principles are complementary and balance each other, as is physically depicted by the hand-sign.

3. An academic interpretation: the open hand stands for academic learning, the clenched fist for martial prowess. The composite hand-sign thus declares that arts and letters and martial arts are mutually supporting aspects of human endeavor and are not to be separated, in order that the balance so created may bring stability to society.

One use of the Black Tiger pai hand-sign is described and illustrated in chapter four.

4 the black tiger
sequence of techniques

THIS CHAPTER DEALS exclusively with the prearranged solo exercise (lien tao-chien), that is, the entire sequence of techniques of the Black Tiger fighting art. This sequence is meant to be practiced as a whole, but for the convenience of novice trainees it has been divided into parts: the opening, seven action groups, and the closing.

Each of the nine parts into which the solo exercise has been divided is fully illustrated by photographs. The trainee must, of course, have the contents of the preceding chapters clearly in mind before beginning the sequence of actions. Questions about mechanical actions that are not elaborately detailed here may be resolved by referring to earlier chapters.

The Western trainee is unlikely to have the guidance of a master who can supervise his training. Therefore it is recommended that he depend on a training partner who can read the descriptions of the actions that he is required to make. This verbal method of instruction can be dispensed with entirely when the trainee has attained the ability to move from one stance and posture to the next without hesitation and can perform the entire sequence of techniques from memory.

The discerning reader will notice that sometimes the text and the photographs illustrating the text appear to be in disagreement. This is caused by the great difficulty of trying to capture photographically the specific actions described in the text, rather than by any error in the performance of the technique. Whenever such a discrepancy appears, depend on the text to resolve the problem.

As you train, bear in mind that the benefit of daily training accumulates. It is far better to train a little every day than to train for long periods on just a few days a week.

opening

1. Stand with feet together, arms bent with elbows ba[?]
fists clenched, knuckles down, at chest level. Look sligh[?]
in a left-front direction (fig. 1).

2. Open the hands, rotating them palms down, and s[?]
press them downward until the arms are fully extended
along your sides (figs. 2–4).

3. Clench the fists again, knuckles up, raising them s[?]
along the sides to chest level, turning the knuckles dow[?]
ward (figs. 5–7).

4. Step forward with the left foot, toes turned inward
and assume a left lunge stance; at the same time open [?]
hands and extend both arms forward at shoulder level,
hands about a handspan apart, palms and knife-edges [?]
the hands to the front (fig. 8).

BEGIN HERE

● KEYPOINTS ●

REF. FIG. 8

REF. FIGS. 9–10

Curl the fingers to touch the thumbs and form a beak-
with each hand; at the same time move your arms in
e sweep to the rear at shoulder level, as though
ming breast stroke. Clench the fists, then turn them
les down; bring them to the sides at chest level as
lide the right foot up next to the left foot (figs. 9–12).
Move the left foot to the left, sinking down into a
-riding stance, and simultaneously thrust-punch with
fists, knuckles up, directly to the sides at shoulder
(figs. 13–15).

REF. FIGS. 15–16

REF. FIGS. 16–17

1. Pivot on the heel of your left foot so that the toes point to the left, and turn your upper body to the left. Maintain your arms extended at shoulder level (fig. 16) but open the fists. Turn 90 degrees to the left, keeping the left arm in a fixed position, but rotate the left palm counterclockwise so that it faces upward. At the same time swing the right arm in a wide arc to the front just above shoulder level, keeping the open hand palm down. Bring the right hand over the left about a handspan away, as if holding a large ball. Simultaneously with the movement of the right arm, shift your weight onto the left leg and raise the right leg, bent at the knee, bringing the instep of the right foot behind the left knee to assume a right balancing stance (fig. 17).

2. While standing on your left leg, bring the heels of the hands together as if catching the enemy's fist (fig. 18). Execute the lock-turning action to bring the left hand above the right hand. As your left hand comes over the right, step back onto the right leg and assume a left lunge stance (figs. 19, 20). Form a beak-hand with your left hand, as if to hook the enemy's attacking arm near his wrist; at the same time, lower both arms until the hands reach groin level, as if bringing the enemy's captured arm downward (figs. 21–23).

Continue without a break in rhythm by simultaneously sweeping both arms back to an open position, the right arm coming high overhead and behind you, palm open, facing the right, while the left arm, as if sweeping the enemy's captured arm to the left, comes down well behind you, hand held in a beak-hand. Do this while shifting your weight back over your right leg. Stand fully on the right leg, raising your left leg, bent at the knee, as you place the sole of the left foot on the inner right thigh above the knee to assume a left balancing stance (figs. 24–28).

3. Step forward with the left leg (fig. 29). Shift your weight onto that leg, assume a left lunge stance, and twist your body to the left. At the same time sweep the right arm forward in a wide arc down to the front, turning the palm up as the hand comes to chest level in front of you. Simultaneously move the left arm, bending it at the elbow, and bring the clenched left fist, knuckles down, to the side at chest level (figs. 30–32).

4. Continue without a pause by raising the right hand, palm open and up to the left front above face level while twisting even more to the left. Rotate the right arm counterclockwise to turn the palm downward and outward, and at the same time withdraw the right arm until the clenched fist comes alongside the right temple. Twist your body to the right as you draw back the right arm and deliver a forward thrust-punch at shoulder level with the left fist (figs. 33–35).

action group

2

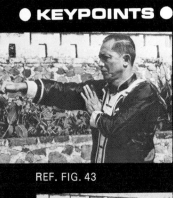

REF. FIG. 43

REF. FIG. 45

1. Keeping your feet in place, twist your body to the le and swing the right arm, knuckles of the right fist rotatin forward, circularly to the front in an outer forearm block action made at head level. Simultaneously withdraw the left fist, knuckles down, to the side at chest level (figs. 36–

2. Pivot the left foot on the heel to the left, and point your toes directly forward (fig. 39).

3. Deliver a forward snap-kick with the instep of the ri foot at groin level, as if kicking up under the enemy's testicles. At the same time, thrust-punch forward with th left fist at face level, pulling back the right arm until the clenched fist, knuckles down, comes to the side at chest level (fig. 40).

4. Step forward and down with the right foot (fig. 41). Deliver a right forward thrust-punch to the front at ches level as you shift your weight onto the right leg, and ass a right lunge stance to reinforce the blow. At the same ti withdraw the left arm so that it takes a protective positic across the body at solar-plexus level, the hand held with palm open and facing the right biceps (figs. 42, 43).

5. Step back with the left foot and shift your weight onto that leg; maintain your arm positions (fig. 44). At the same instant withdraw the right leg a bit and float that foot as you forcefully lower your hips and come into a right ready stance to reinforce a downward blow made with your right back-fist, knuckles down, to groin level, as if striking the shinbone of the enemy's kicking leg in front of you. Your left hand extends only as far as the inside of the right elbow, where it is placed, palm up, under the elbow joint to support it (fig. 45).

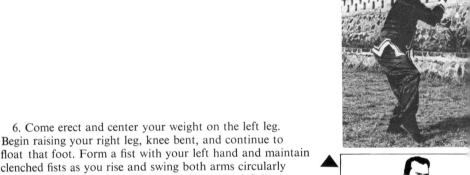

6. Come erect and center your weight on the left leg. Begin raising your right leg, knee bent, and continue to float that foot. Form a fist with your left hand and maintain clenched fists as you rise and swing both arms circularly upward to the rear (fig. 46). Stand fully on the left leg in a right balancing stance. Extend the left arm high overhead behind your body, the thumb of that fist facing forward, while the right arm, upon reaching the level of your left shoulder, delivers a blow with the back-fist circularly over, forward, and down across the top of your raised right thigh, as if striking against the shinbone of the enemy's kicking leg (fig. 47).

7. Leap into the air, turning in place 90 degrees to your right. Land in the horse-riding stance and beat both back-fists downward at groin level, as if double-striking the shinbone of the enemy's kicking leg, keeping your elbows close to your sides (figs. 48, 49).

BEGIN HERE

8. Look to your left (your frontal direction before the jump in the previous maneuver; fig. 50). Keeping your feet in place, come erect and swing both arms together in a large arc, back and up to your right (fig. 51). As you come erect, shift your weight onto the forward left leg, stretching the rear right leg, to assume a left lunge stance. With this shift forward, swing the left arm up and over into a forward overhead-downward blow made with the back-fist at top-of-head level (the hammer blow). Your right hand, fist clenched, knuckles back and down, is raised high above head level behind you (fig. 52).

9. Keeping your feet in place, twist your upper body to the left and deliver an overhead-downward blow of the right back-fist in front of you to top-of-head level (the whip blow). Withdraw your left arm, fist clenched, knuckles down, to your side at chest level (figs. 53, 54).

action group 3

BEGIN HERE

HERE THE
CAMERA ANGLE
SHIFTS

1. While in a left lunge stance, keep your clenched right fist at face level in front of you, but slide your left hand, palm open and facing upward, forward to cross over the inside of the right wrist (fig. 55).

2. Still maintaining a clenched right fist, turn the left hand palm down and form a beak-hand (fig. 56). Open the right fist and lower both arms, bringing the hands to knee level (fig. 57). Sweep your right hand, palm upward, down

ck; at the same time your left beak-hand o the left behind you). Pivot both feet to ht and twist your o the right to shift ʋeight onto the right etch your left leg me into a right lunge (fig. 59). Continue g to your left, and same time sweep ht arm circularly nd up to shoulder) the right, with the. acing away from the Simultaneously the

left arm, hand held in a beak-hand, sweeps up and back behind your left hip at hip level (fig. 60).

3. Maintain the right lunge stance and the position of your right arm, but swing your left arm, palm open and up, across the front of your body to bring the left hand to the inner side of the right shoulder, palm facing your neck (figs. 61, 62).

4. Continue looking to the left over your left shoulder; then step the

left leg a long step forward, ahead of your bent right leg (fig. 63). Pivoting on the right foot, turn 180 degrees to your right and come into a right lunge stance again. Your right arm remains extended to the right at shoulder level, palm forward, while once more you sweep a left beak-hand back behind you (figs. 64, 65. Here the camera angle shifts to a position in front of the performer; action continues from that perspective).

HERE THE CAMERA ANGL SHIFTS

Shift your weight to the left and assume a horse-riding stance. At the same time raise the left arm, bent at the elbow, and roll that arm upward to bring the forearm into a protective position, hand held in a fist, thumb down, in front of your forehead,

while your right arm delivers a downward blow with the bottom-fist to the right side at hip level (fig. 66).

5. Reassume a right lunge stance by shifting your weight over the right leg, pivoting the left foot in a clockwise direction

and fully stretching the left leg. Face the right front; at the same time extend your arms forw in the direction you ar now facing. Lower the arm to solar-plexus lev and rotate the fist cou clockwise until the knu face your left. Raise th

right arm and bring the fist to face level, knuckles facing your right (fig. 67). (Here the camera angle shifts to a position directly in front of the performer; action will continue from that perspective.) Unclench the fists. Cross the right arm over the left at the wrists, the palms of both hands open, at chest level in front of you (fig. 68).

6. Press the heels of the hands together and execute the lock-turning action to bring the left hand over the right (figs. 69–73).

7. Clench the fists (fig. 74). Separate the hands forcefully by drawing the left arm back and down, the left fist, knuckles down, coming to your side at chest level. At the same time keep the right arm extended as you sweep it back and upward in a rolling manner, high overhead but in front of the body, rotating the fist counterclockwise until the knuckles face the rear (figs. 75, 76).

8. Stamp your right foot forcefully to the ground, turning the toes outward to the right as you twist your upper body to the right and carry your extended and raised right arm back high overhead behind you. Your left fist remains at your side at chest level (fig. 77).

9. Step forward with the left foot and assume a left lunge stance. Twist your upper body to the left and deliver a forward, overhead-downward blow of the right back-fist to top-of-head level (the whip blow). The left fist remains at your side at chest level (figs. 78, 79).

1. (Here the camera angle shifts to a position on the left of the performer; action will continue from that perspective.) Hold yourself in the left lunge stance. Keeping your feet in place, twist your body to the right and deliver a forward thrust-punch at shoulder level with the left fist. The right arm is bent, rotated counterclockwise, and withdrawn, elbow first, close to the body. As the right fist comes alongside your head, strike to the rear at head level, pivoting your arm on the elbow, hand held in a bottom-fist with knuckles up (fig. 80).

2. Step back slightly with the right foot, shift your weight onto that foot, and floa the left foot; at the sar time crouch and bring left foot back to the rig As you crouch, swing left arm, fist clenched and thumb uppermost, downward to knee leve but maintain the positi of your right arm (fig.

...nue without a break ...vement, rising out ...: crouch; swing your ...m, fist clenched and ...les down, back and ...ross your chest; ...ain the position of ...right arm. As your ...t comes to head level, ...orward with your ...ot and shift your ...t forward into a left ...stance to reinforce ...livery of an over- ...downward blow to ...ft with your left ...fist at top-of-head ...the hammer blow); ...ain the position of ...right arm (figs. 82–84). ...eeping your feet in ...quickly twist your ...to the left and deliver ...t back-fist to top-of- ...level in an overhead- ...ward way (whip blow).

Draw the left arm back and high overhead behind you, fist clenched and knuckles to the rear (fig. 85).

4. Momentarily maintain the stance shown in figure 85, but lower your extended right arm in front of your body, fist at groin level with the knuckles down (fig. 86).

5. Pivot the left foot on the heel to the left so that the toes point in the direction you are facing, and deliver a high forward snap-kick to chin level with the trailing right leg, using the upper portion of the toes as the striking surface. At the height of the kick, stand fully on the left foot, heel off the ground. Your right arm remains in a protective position at groin level, fist held with thumb up, and your left arm maintains its high position behind you, fist clenched with knuckles facing back (fig. 87).

6. Maintain the protective position of the right fist and the raised left arm as you replace the right foot on the ground, stepping well forward to assume a right lunge stance, with the left leg fully stretched behind you (fig. 88).

7. Keeping your feet in place, look left, unclench the right fist, turning it palm up, and begin raising the right arm in an extended position in front of your body. At the same time twist your body to the left, bend and lower the left arm, and bring the left fist to your side at chest level, knuckles down (fig. 89). Continue raising the right arm, rolling that arm so that the knuckles face up, until it is at forehead level in front of your body (fig. 90).

When the right arm, hand held palm down, is in that high position, deliver a forward thrust-punch with your left fist at shoulder level. Keep your feet in place as you punch, but twist your body to the right and withdraw your right arm alongside your head near the right temple, fist clenched and thumb down (figs. 91–93).

8. Shift from a right lunge stance to a left lunge

92

REF. FIG. 95

94

95

99

100

stance by twisting to the left; pivot both feet counterclockwise and fully stretch the right leg. Deliver a right bottom-fist to rib level as you shift, and at the same time

withdraw the left arm to a protective position in front of your body. Place your left palm, fingers pointing forward and up, directly against the inside of the striking right arm just

below the elbow joint support it (figs. 94, 95

9. Step circularly fc with the right foot (se arrow in fig. 95). At t same time slide your hand, palm open and

HERE THE
CAMERA ANGLE
SHIFTS

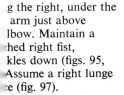

g the right, under the
arm just above
lbow. Maintain a
hed right fist,
kles down (figs. 95,
Assume a right lunge
e (fig. 97).

10. Keep your feet in place as you twist your body to the right. Withdraw the right arm, bringing that fist to your side at chest level, knuckles down. At the same time slide the left arm forward and up the undersurface of the right arm, palm and knife-edge of the left hand forward (fig. 98). (Here the camera angle shifts to a position in front of the performer; action will continue from that perspective.) Figure 99 shows the completed action.

11. Shift your weight more onto the advanced right leg, stretching the rear left leg, and twist your upper body to the left as you move the right elbow in a horizontal arc forward and across the front of your body. Rotate the right fist into a knuckles-up position to focus that blow at solar-plexus level; withdraw your left arm, palm open, and drive the right forearm, just below the elbow, forcefully into the palm of your left hand (fig. 100).

12. Quickly bring your right arm over in an arc, pivoting the arm on the elbow, and deliver a forward overhead-downward blow with the right back-fist to top-of-head level (the hammer blow). Move your left hand to a protective position at chest level, palm down, under the right arm just above the elbow joint (fig. 101).

13. Pivot the right foot on the heel to the right so that the toes point in the direction you are facing. Twist the body to the right; the left foot pivots on the toes and advances slightly but not in line with the advanced right foot. Open the right fist and turn the palm down, then withdraw the right arm and extend the left arm forward, palm and knife-edge of the hand to the front (fig. 102). Continue to twist to the right, and as your arms separate, sink down onto the left knee (figs. 103, 104). Bring the left

94

knee behind and outside the ankle bone of the right foot, and sit on the upraised left heel. In the kneeling posture both arms are extended. The left arm is well forward, inclining upward to a position at the left front; the left palm and knife-edge of the hand face your front, fingers slanting back to the right. The right arm extends downward to the rear, palm open and facing down (fig. 105).

14. Rise quickly onto the right leg and deliver a whirl-wind-kick with the left foot aimed at head level, using the instep-shin area as a striking surface; spin 180 degrees to your right as you kick, and come into a left tiger stance (figs. 106–9).

action group

5

From the left tiger in figure 109, swing foot backward in a arc to your left (see in fig. 110); assume lunge stance, but looking to your left. same time fold the n across the chest to ht, bringing that palm open, into a protective position facing the inside of the right shoulder. Lower the right arm slightly (figs. 110–12).

2. Shift your weight onto the left leg, moving the right leg behind the left (see arrow in fig. 113). At the same time sweep both hands to the left, parallel to the ground in front of the body, palms open and facing away from you. Sweep the left hand back to the left side at face level, palm out, then fold the right arm across the body at chest level, the right palm at the left shoulder and facing down-ward (figs. 113–15).

REF. FIGS. 127–28

3. As you maintain this crossed-leg stance, change arm positions. Lower the extended left arm, palm down, to hip level, and at the same time raise and extend the right arm upward in a counterclockwise arc to your right-front, high above your head, palm open and facing away from your body (figs. 116, 117).

4. From the crossed-leg stance look more to your left and continue to move your arms by reversing their arcs. The right arm is bent and lowered, palm down, in a coun clockwise arc, to a position near the left shoulder, arm parallel to the ground. Raise the extended left arm, rotati the palm upward, until both arms have come again to shoulder level (figs. 118, 119).

5. Swing your arms circularly, left arm clockwise and right arm counterclockwise, by raising the left arm and lowering the right (figs. 120, 121). Both hands describe la arcs in front of the body: the left hand rises, palm up, in big circle overhead and then, with palm down, comes to position in front of the body at groin level; the right hand moves downward until, when at the level of the solar plexus, it is rolled upward to bring the right hand, palm open and facing outward, into a protective position in fro of but above the level of the head (figs. 122, 123). At the instant that the arms come into the positions shown in

e 120, shift your weight onto the right leg and step the
eg wide to your left-rear corner to fully stretch that leg
arrows in figs. 120, 121). Come into a right lunge
e as shown in figures 122 and 123, but continue to look
ur left.

From the platform right leg, leap high into the air to
left; the left leg leads as you turn 90 degrees to the
Deliver a forward double snap-kick (left foot, then right
while in midair, to groin and chin levels, respectively,
the instep or the upper portion of the toes as
ng surfaces (figs. 124–26). Land on the left leg and
a long step forward with the right foot. Both hands,
in fists, are positioned at the sides of the body (fig. 127).
the forward step, go directly into a right lunge stance
leliver a right thrust-punch to chest level. The left arm
ught into a protective position at solar-plexus level
the left hand at the right biceps, palm open and facing
ody (fig. 128).

Keeping both feet in place, but pivoting on them a bit
e left, shift your weight to the left leg and turn your
r body 90 degrees to the left to assume a left lunge
e. With the shift, swing both extended arms across the
to the left at shoulder level. Bring the hands together,
s open and facing each other. Position the hands at

● KEYPOINT ●

REF. FIG. 133

137

138

e level, fingers touching and pointing upward, to form a
angle in front of you (figs. 129, 130).

8. Step the right leg behind the left (see arrow in fig. 130)
d begin to sink down as you raise both arms upward a
ort distance, then, separating the hands, swing the arms
opposite directions, palms down, in big arcs outward to
e sides and downward to a position in front of your body
. 131). Sink fully down onto the right knee, which is
sitioned outside the ankle bone of the left foot. Sit on
e upraised right heel. Bring the arms upward in front of
u in a circular movement until the fingertips touch once
ain, hands palm to palm at face level in front of you
gs. 132, 133).

9. Maintain the crossed-leg stance as you rise to an erect
sition (fig. 134), and extend both arms widely outward
d up to your sides, palms open and facing outward (fig.
5). Keep your arms in this extended position for balance
you shift your weight onto the right leg; then swing the
. leg upward to your left to deliver a forward thrust-kick
solar-plexus level, using the heel as the striking surface
s. 136, 137). After the kick, step the left foot to the
und, taking a long step in the direction of the kick just
de. Twist your body to the left and extend the left arm,
d open, palm facing forward, as you bring your right
, knuckles down, to your side at chest level. Assume a
lunge stance (fig. 138).

99

1. Maintain a left lunge stance. Form a fist with your left hand, turning the thumb uppermost (fig. 139). Pivot the left foot on the heel to the left, toes pointing outward, then step forward with the right foot while keeping the left arm extended in front of the body. When the right foot comes to the ground ahead of you, assume a right lunge stance and deliver a forward right thrust-punch at chin level. At the same time withdraw the left arm and bring it into a protective position across the body, palm open and near the right shoulder (figs. 140, 141).

2. Turn your head to the left. Shift your weight onto your left leg and bring the right foot up to the left. At the same time swing the knife-edge of the left hand, palm open and down, in an upward arc to a high position at your left so that the palm faces upward; withdraw the right fist, knuckles dow to your side at chest le (figs. 142–44).

3. Shift your weight completely onto the rig leg and deliver a left forward thrust-kick to chin level, using the he a striking surface (fig. Step down immediately with the kicking left le and take a long step forward in the direction of the kick. Come into left lunge stance, left a

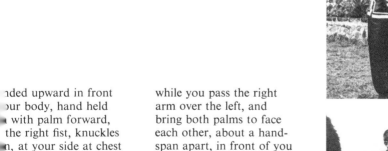

...ded upward in front ...ur body, hand held ... with palm forward, the right fist, knuckles ...n, at your side at chest (fig. 146).

Shift your weight onto left leg and bring the ...ng right foot up next . Twist your upper ... to the left. Unclench ...ight fist and extend ... arms in front of you. ...er the left arm to ...-plexus level, turning hand palm upward

while you pass the right arm over the left, and bring both palms to face each other, about a hand-span apart, in front of you (fig. 147). Raise both hands to face level, and press the heels of the hands together (fig. 148). While standing with feet together, execute the lock-turning action and bring the left hand uppermost (figs. 149, 150).

BEGIN HERE

Form a left beak-hand, then sweep both arms downward and back: sweep your left hand to the left rear, hand held in beak-hand formation, while your right arm, hand open, is swung down, then up and back to a position high overhead and to the side of your body, palm facing forward (figs. 151–53).

5. Shift your weight fully onto the right leg while maintaining your arms in their relative positions. Deliver a left forward thrust-kick to chin level, using the heel as a striking surface (fig. 154). Return the left foot to the ground, and take a long step forward in the direction of the kick (fig. 155). Come into a left lunge stance. Raise the left arm, fully extended, upward to the front above head level, hand held in a fist with knuckles facing back; the right hand, held in a fist with knuckles down, is brought to your side at chest level (fig. 156).

6. Slide the trailing right leg up to and behind the platform left leg (see arrow in fig. 156), and quickly shift your weight onto the right leg. Leap off the right leg and jump forward in the direction are facing. Keep your left arm in its high protective position in front of you, and your right hand, held in a fist, at your side at chest level (fig. 157). Land in a left bow-drawing stance, but maintain your arm positions (fig. 158).

153

157

▼

158

▲

▲

REF. FIGS. 156–58 ▲

action group

7

1. From the left bow-drawing stance, bring the advanced and outstretched left foot back to the platform right foot (see arrow in fig. 159); rise and leap off the right foot high into the air, but jump in place—do not leap forward. Turn 180 degrees to the left. While turning in the air, execute a low roundhouse-kick at knee level, using the right instep-shin area as a striking surface, as if aiming behind the enemy's advanced kn to try to hook him off hi advanced leg through the momentum generated by your jump. Unclench bo fists, raise your right arm high overhead, and bring your left hand, palm dov into a protective position in front of your body at solar-plexus level (fig. 16 Land on your left leg an drop down into a right bow-drawing stance. Yo raised right arm, hand n reclenched in a fist, chop downward to knee level, the outer forearm being used as a striking surfac your left arm, hand ope sweeps outward and upward, palm forward, your left-front (fig. 161). Keeping your feet in pla immediately twist your

y to the right, and
1 the right hand held in
:ak-hand sweep your
t arm backward to
r right-rear; your
arm maintains its
ective position. With
1 your arms extended
he sides at shoulder
l, maintain the right
-drawing stance; your
y approximates the
De of the letter *T* (fig.
).
. Rise out of this deep
ice and shift your
ght forward onto the
t leg. Assume a right
ge stance. Simulta-
usly raise both arms
vard and circularly
vard, keeping them
nded, palms open
facing down (fig. 163).
tinue raising both arms

until your right arm is at
forehead level, palm facing
your right with thumb
down, and your left arm,
palm open and also
facing the right with
thumb up, is at throat level
(fig. 164). With your arms
in these positions, clench
both fists as if seizing the
enemy's attacking arm, and
pull backward and down
with both arms. Bring both
fists to your right side, the
right fist at chest level, the
left fist at hip level, the
knuckles of both fists
facing down (figs. 165,
166).
    3. Maintaining the posi-
tions of your fists, shift
your weight onto the right
leg and step the left foot
forward into a position
as close as possible in

front of the right foot,
the toes of the right foot
turned in to your left so
that the left foot points
in the direction of your
right-front corner (see
arrow in fig. 166; fig. 167).
Shift your weight onto
your left leg.
    4. Using your left leg as
a platform, deliver a
forward double thrust-
punch circularly up and
over to the front as you
bend forward from the
hips. Your upper right fist,
thumb down, punches at
face level, while the left
fist, thumb up, aims at the
level of the solar plexus.
Thrust your right leg to the
rear as a counterbalance;
the position of your body
approximates a *T* (figs.
168, 169).

5. Replace the right fo
on the ground by taking
long step to your rear,
and assume a left lunge
stance. Both arms, hand
clenched in fists with
knuckles down, are bent
at the elbow and held in
front of the body (fig. 1

6. Pivot the right foot
on the heel to the right,
and turn 180 degrees to
the right by pivoting in
place. As you turn, shift
your weight onto your
now advanced right foo
and momentarily assum
right lunge stance as sho
in figure 171. Without
pausing, take a long step
forward with your left
foot (see arrow in fig. 1

106

after the left foot
…es to the ground, pivot
…hat foot to turn 180
…rees in a clockwise
…ction; do this by
…nging your right leg
… wide arc to the right
…ind you as shown in
…re 172. Come into a
… lunge stance, facing
…r original direction.
… this time your arms,
…ds held in fists with
…ckles down, maintain
…r positions in front of
…r body (fig. 173).

(Here the camera
…le shifts to a position
…he right side of the
…ormer; action will
…tinue from that
…spective.) Thrust-

punch in opposite
directions with both fists
simultaneously; the left
fist thrusts forward at
shoulder level, while the
right fist thrusts backward
at face level (fig. 174).

8. Pivot the left foot
to the left, toes pointing
forward, and twist your
upper body to the left.
Maintain the position of
your left arm, hand held
in a fist, in front of your
body. Shift your weight
onto your left leg and begin
to bring the trailing right
leg forward as you swing
your right arm, hand open
with palm down, forward
in a wide arc parallel to
the ground at shoulder

level; begin to lower your
left arm (fig. 175). Bring
your right leg forward and
assume a right balancing
stance, placing the instep
of your right foot behind
your left knee. At the same
time, continue to swing
your right arm forward,
bringing it to a position
in front of your body at
face level. Pass your right
hand, palm down, over
and above your left hand,
which is now held open,
palm up, at solar-plexus
level. Balance fully on your
left leg and hold both arms
in extended positions in
front of you, palms facing
each other about a hand-
span apart (fig. 176).

9. While standing in the right balancing stance, bring the
heels of your hands together (fig. 177). Execute the lock-
turning action to bring the left hand above the right (fig.
178). As your left hand comes uppermost, step back with
your right leg and assume a left lunge stance (figs. 179, 180).
Form the beak-hand with your left hand, then lower both
your arms until the hands reach groin level (fig. 181).

Continue without a break in movement by simultaneously sweeping both arms back into an open position the right arm coming to a high position overhead and behind you, palm facing the right, while the left arm comes to a low position well behind you, hand held in a beak-hand. With these arm actions shift your weight onto your rear right leg (figs. 182–85). Assume a left balancing stance by standing fully on your right leg and raising your left leg, bent at the knee, and placing the sole of your left foot on the inner thigh of the right leg above the knee (figs. 186, 187).

187

186

185

1

BEGIN HERE

182

closing

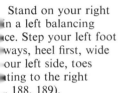

Stand on your right
in a left balancing
ce. Step your left foot
ways, heel first, wide
our left side, toes
ting to the right
. 188, 189).

Shift your weight onto
r left leg and pivot on
foot, turning 90 de-
s to the right as you
v the right foot back
gside the left; bring
arms, bent at the
ws, palms open and
n, in front of your body
190). Make the hand-
of the Shantung Black
r pai as you stand erect
heels together. Do this
lenching the right fist,
ckles up, at chest level
ont of your body, and
ringing the left palm,
ng downward, above
right fist (fig. 191).

Draw both arms
othly back, clenching
eft hand into a fist.
tion the fists, knuckles
n, at your sides at
t level (fig. 192).

Open the fists; rotate
palms inward and
nward (fig. 193).

Press both hands,
is down, slowly down-
d to fully extend your
s along your sides (figs.
195).

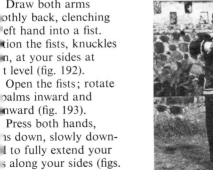

5 practical applications

ONCE YOU HAVE BECOME PROFICIENT in the solo method of perform-   **113**
ing the sequence of techniques in the Black Tiger fighting art, it is only
natural that you should want to learn how to apply these techniques as
self-defense measures. Many self-defense applications will suggest themselves to you as your skill increases, and you will perhaps develop some
effective skills on your own. In this chapter you will find some examples of
how the Black Tiger techniques can be applied in self-defense.

It is important to realize that this chapter cannot possibly deal with all
types of self-defense situations and their responses that may occur. Rather,
what is presented here is a small but representative sample of the kind of
unarmed hand-to-hand encounters that may occur in everyday life. The
Black Tiger responses presented as useful in dealing with these emergency
situations were selected because they are so simple and efficient that the
average person can perform them. The authors further believe that by the
selection of techniques that are related in nature, you will benefit greatly
through having to practice similar actions repeatedly and will become more
expert in a shorter length of time than would be possible if you were left
to wander through a maze of dissimilar and difficult techniques.

For the reader's convenience, the practical applications in this chapter
have been divided into two groups, classical and modern. The classical
applications deal with the defender, garbed in traditional Chinese dress,
assuming stances and postures and performing actions precisely as they are
performed in the prearranged order (tao-chien) of the Black Tiger art. In
this group the defender does not deviate from what may be called the classical or pure form of the art. In the modern applications, however, the uti-
lization of Black Tiger techniques for self-defense is not bound by such
formalities. This group deals with the defender dressed in modern clothing
and, of course, trained in the techniques of the Black Tiger art as he might
meet an emergency situation that has been suddenly thrust upon him. His
responses are made in a natural manner, such as might be improvised on
the spur of the moment.

A word of caution is necessary before you begin your study and practice
of these applications. No system has yet been devised that will unfailingly
solve every combative situation that its exponent may face. The exponent
of the Black Tiger fighting art must bear this in mind; in all fairness, the
authors strongly advise him, when he faces a threat by an assailant, to use
only those portions of the Black Tiger art in which he is expert, and further, to use only those techniques that are appropriate to his situation.

Situation: The defender stands in a left balancing stance facing an enemy who is menacing her with clenched fists while in a left stance (fig. 196).

Response: As the enemy steps forward and reaches with his right hand to clutch at the defender's throat or claw her face, the defender steps her raised left leg directly forward toward the oncoming attacker, heel first and toes turned inward, and assumes a left lunge stance. At the same time she brings her right arm across her body, hand held with the palm open and facing her body at throat level. She passes this arm under the enemy's attacking right arm near his wrist; she also brings her left hand, formed in a fist, to her side at chest level (figs. 197, 198). The defender quickly grasps the enemy's attacking right arm with her right hand, held thumb down, from the outside near the enemy's wrist (fig. 199). She then pull the enemy's right arm upward toward her right-rear corner, twisting her body to the right to reinforce this action, as can be seen in figure 200. At the same time she delivers a forward thrust-punch with her left fist to the assailant's solar plexus (fig. 201).

classical application

1

● KEYPOINTS ●

REF. FIG. 199

REF. FIG. 201

Keypoints: The defender must step
forward only at the very moment that the
enemy reaches out with his right hand to
attack. Details of the defender's actions
as she grasps the enemy's right wrist and
delivers the thrust-punch are found in
Action Group 1, figures 28–35.

classical application

116

2

Situation: This situation is a logical continuation of the preceding situation, and might occur if the defender's punching action is ineffective. Here the enemy, even after having been struck by the defender, continues to attack by pulling his captured right arm free of the defender's grasp and by grasping or clawing at the defender's throat or face with his left hand (figs. 202, 203).

Response: As the enemy frees his right arm and starts to use his left hand to attack, the defender, who is in a left lunge stance, twists her body to her left and delivers an outer forearm block with her right arm against the outside of the enemy's left arm near his wrist. At the same time the defender withdraws her left arm and brings her left fist to her side at chest level (figs. 204–6). The defender pivots her left foot on the heel to point the toes directly at the enemy, and immediately shifts her weight forward fully onto the advanced left leg (fig. 207). Simultaneously with this shift of weight she delivers a right forward snap-kick up under the enemy's groin, using the instep of her right foot as the striking surface, and a forward thrust-punch with her left fist to the enemy's chin. With these two actions she withdraws her right fist to her side at chest level (fig. 208).

Keypoints: The defender must not resist the assailant's attempt to free his captured right arm, for fear of losing her balance and falling forward. Details of the defender's block, kick, and punch will be found in Action Group 2, figures 36–40.

classical application

3

Situation: An enemy approaches the defender in a menacing manner. The defender assumes a left tiger stance, quartering the left side of her body into t enemy (fig. 209). The enemy steps forwar with his right leg, grasps the defender's outstretched left arm near the wrist with left hand, and attempts to deliver a blow his right fist to the defender's head (fig. 2

Response: When the enemy grasps her lef arm with his left hand, the defender keep her feet in place but leans backward over her rear right leg and brings her right ha

n open and facing frontward, into a
ective position in front of her face (fig.
. Swiftly the defender grasps the enemy's
:king right arm near the wrist with her
t hand, held thumb down; she stretches
left arm forward and allows the enemy to
itain his grip on her left wrist (fig. 212).
lenly the defender draws back her
nded left arm to her rear, under the
ny's captured right arm; the attacker's
hand grasp is broken as his left hand
es under his own right armpit.
iediately, the defender places her now
left hand, palm down, on top of the
ny's right elbow from the outside. The
nder quickly shifts her weight forward to
k the enemy's balance in a forward
:tion (fig. 213). She does this by a
bined forward push and downward pull
·r right hand on the enemy's captured
arm, and a forward and downward
of her left hand against the enemy's
elbow. At the same time the defender
ps her extended left leg forcefully
ward against the enemy's right knee
, using the back of her knee joint as a
ing surface (figs. 214–17).

oints: Various elements taken from
on Group 5 are included in this

response. It is important to understand
that though the defender may appear to the
enemy to be indifferent to the situation when
she adopts a stance that quarters into the
enemy's line of advance, the defender
remains alert and keeps visual contact with
the enemy. The timing of the evasion of the
enemy's blow to the head, and of the
defender's interception and grasp of that
attacking arm, is critical. Study the details
of the grasp and the very obvious shift of
weight to the rear that the defender must
make to avoid that blow. The defender must
withdraw her left arm while pushing forward
against the enemy's captured right arm and
at the same time must shift her weight
forward without weighting her advanced
left leg. She literally throws her weight
against the enemy's upper body, transmitting
that force through his captured right arm.
The enemy will quite naturally attempt to
disengage his right leg to regain his balance,
but if the defender's arm and hand actions
against the enemy's captured right arm are
made correctly, he will fail.

● KEYPOINTS ●

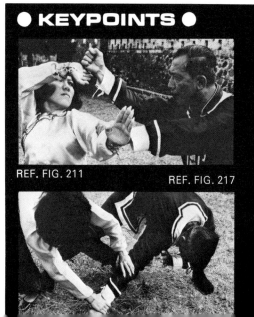

REF. FIG. 211   REF. FIG. 217

classical application

4

Situation: The defender is in a left ready stance as the enemy approaches with his fists clenched. The enemy steps forward with his right foot and attempts to punch the defender in the face (figs. 218, 219).

Response: At the instant of the enemy's right-hand punch, the defender pivots to her left on her right foot and steps her left foot directly behind her. At the same time she brings both hands into a protective position in front of her, the right hand open, the left hand in a fist at solar-plexus level (fig. 220). The defender quickly grasps the attacker's right wrist from the outside with her right hand, held thumb down, and brings her left fist to her side at chest level (fig. 221). Maintaining her grasp of the enemy's right wrist, and also keeping her feet in place, the defender shifts her weight onto her advanced right leg and breaks the enemy's balance forward and downward she does this by the combined actions of a pull with her right hand downward to her right against the assailant's captured right arm and a downward pushing action of her left hand, placed on top of the enemy's right elbow (figs. 222, 223). The defender keeps both her hands on the enemy's outstretched right arm, still forcing it downward, and attempts to deliver a forward thrust-kick with her retreated left leg, using the heel as a striking surface against the enemy's right knee joint (fig. 224).

The enemy, however, manages to withdraw his right leg, stepping it far behind him, and thus avoids this kick (fig. 225). The defender then steps her left foot down, heel first, and continues to counterattack by attempting another forward thrust-kick with her right foot, using the heel of that foot as a striking surface against the instep of the enemy's now advanced left foot (figs. 226, 227). The enemy escapes this kick by withdrawing his advanced left leg, moving it backward in a long step to his rear; he also manages to adopt a more erect posture. The defender pursues her counterattack by stepping her right foot down, heel first; she shifts her weight more onto her now advanced right leg, the toes of her right foot pointing to her right (fig. 228). She releases both her hands from the enemy's right arm and drops down over her platform right leg to execute a low roundhouse-kick in a clockwise direction with her left leg, using the instep of that foot as a striking surface against the back of the enemy's right leg near his knee (fig. 229). The enemy escapes this kick by pivoting on his rear left foot, and whirls around to his left to face the defender, who is now in a left bow-drawing stance (fig. 230). The defender quickly rises and assumes a left ready stance (fig. 218).

Keypoints: Elements from various action groups in chapter four have been included in this response; their precise identification is not important. The action portrayed here is a variation of Classical Application 3, but it can also be considered an extension of that application in a situation where the defender has not completely broken and gained control over the enemy's balance. The defender must not step forward too quickly after grasping the enemy's right wrist and placing her left hand on top of his right elbow. She must literally throw her weight forward and downward against the enemy's right arm in order to break his balance and pin his advanced foot in place so that her kicks will be effective.

classical application

5

Situation: After assuming a left ready stance at the unsuccessful conclusion of the preceding application, the defender confronts the enemy, who is now closing in on her from a left stance with both fists clenched (fig. 231).

Response: As the assailant steps forward with his right foot and clutches at the defender's face with his right hand, the defender keeps both feet in place but assumes a more erect posture (fig. 232). She brings her right arm upward across her body to the left and grasps the enemy's right wrist from the outside with her right hand, held thumb down; at the same time she withdraws her left fist to her side at chest level (fig. 233). Keeping her feet in place, the defender now shifts her weight onto her advanced left leg and assumes a left lunge stance. Quickly she pulls the attacker's right arm down and back to her right rear; simultaneously she delivers a left forward thrust-punch into the assailant's solar plexus (fig. 234). The enemy pulls his captured right arm free of the defender's grasp and begins to claw her face with his left hand (fig 235). The defender forms a fist with her right hand twists her upper body hard to her left,

delivers an outer forearm block with
right arm against the enemy's
cking left arm near his wrist. At the
e time the defender withdraws her left
o her side at chest level (figs. 236,
. Immediately, the defender shifts her
ht onto her advanced left leg and
ultaneously delivers a right forward
-kick up under the enemy's groin
a left forward thrust-punch to the
ny's chin (fig. 238).

oints: This application is similar to
sical Applications 1 and 2 but is
ormed from a different initial stance.
purpose of this exercise is to tie
her the elements of those early
ications and to use them in a unified
ner. The keypoints for Classical
ications 1 and 2 apply equally to this
tion, except that here the defender
not step forward to meet the
ny's initial attack.

239

modern application

1

Situation: An assailant stands in a left stance, fists clenched, and is trying to punch the defender, who stands facing his attacker head on (fig. 239).

Response: The assailant steps forward with his right foot and delivers a right thrust-punch aimed at the defender's midsection (fig. 240). This attack is neutralized by the defender, who quickly blends with the force of the punch; he steps his left foot backward in a short arc to a position behind his right foot, and simultaneously bends and raises both arms, hands in fists, knuckles down, in front of his body (fig. 241). As the defender's left foot comes into a stable position behind him and he assumes a right lunge stance, he strikes down with the back-fists of both hands simultaneously against the upper surface of the assailant's attacking right arm to block that arm, using the base knuckles of the first two fingers of each hand as striking surfaces (fig. 242). Keeping both arms in a covering position in front of his body, the defender pivots his advanced right foot on the heel so that the toes point directly at his attacker. He then shifts his weight fully onto his right leg and delivers a left forward

...st-kick, using the heel as a striking ...ace, into the right knee joint of the ...ilant (fig. 243). Without a pause the ...nder steps his kicking leg forward to ...ground, shifts his weight onto that ...and delivers a forward snap-kick with ...right foot up under the assailant's ...n, using the instep of the foot as a ...cing surface. At the same time the ...nder lowers his right arm, hand ...ned in a fist, knuckles forward, to a ...ective position in front of his groin ...raises his left arm, hand also held in ...t, knuckles up, to a position high ...head (figs. 244, 245). After delivering ...right forward snap-kick, the defender

● KEYPOINT ●

REF. FIG. 242

replaces his right foot on the ground in front of him (fig. 246). As the assailant falls to the ground, the defender follows up his advantage by delivering a hammer blow with his right back-fist to the top of the assailant's forehead, using the base knuckles of the first two fingers as a striking surface. The defender lunges well forward over his advanced right leg to reinforce the blow; he maintains the high position of his left arm, hand held in a fist (figs. 247, 248).

ypoints: Both back-fists should be ought down against the assailant's acking right arm so that the right ck-fist strikes the assailant's forearm r his elbow joint and the left back-fist kes his wrist or the back of his hand. e forward thrust-kick can be delivered er against the front of the assailant's anced right knee or against the inner e of the knee. Note that the defender ivers this thrust-kick as he bends his ly forward, jutting his buttocks out

backward; he must not throw his head back or lean backward as he kicks. The defender should step his left foot down, heel first, to a position in front of the assailant so that he will be within the correct kicking distance of his next target, the underside of the assailant's groin. Notice that the hammer blow of the defender's right back-fist is a rapid circular action, made upward and over, then downward onto the target; the striking arm pivots on the elbow.

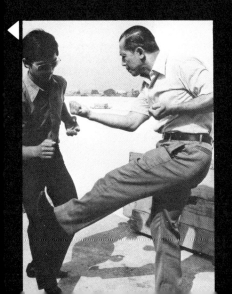

● KEYPOINTS ●

◀ REF. FIGS. 243–45

249

modern application

2

Situation: An assailant closes in on the defender from a left stance, both fists clenched, and is about to strike the defender, who stands directly facing his attacker (fig. 249).

Response: At the instant that the assailant steps forward with his right foot, he swings a roundhouse punch with his right fist, aiming at the left side of the defender's head. The defender keeps both feet in place but leans well back to his right-rear corner to blend with the force of the oncoming punch (fig. 250). The defender quickly brush-blocks the punch

KEYPOINT

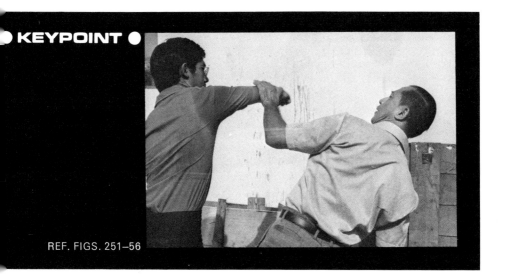

REF. FIGS. 251–56

...mlessly across the front of his body to ...right by using his left hand, palm ...n, against the outside of the assailant's ...cking arm; the defender twists his ...er body to the right to aid this action .. 251). With this twist the defender ...hes the assailant's arm downward with ...left hand, well across the front of the ...ailant's body to the assailant's left, to ...n the assailant's body to the left; at the ...ie time the defender raises his right ...ı, hand formed in a fist, knuckles back, ...his rear (fig. 252). The attack turned ...le, the defender continues to keep his ...hand in contact with the assailant's

right arm, pushing that arm against the assailant's body.
At the same time the defender, keeping both feet in place and pivoting on them, twists his upper body to his left, then shifts his weight well forward over his advanced left leg and delivers a whip blow with his right back-fist to the right side of the assailant's head, using the base knuckles of the first two fingers as a striking surface (figs. 253, 254). As the assailant crumples to the ground the defender follows up his advantage by delivering a roundhouse-kick with his right foot into the assailant's groin, using

the upper portion of the toes as a striking surface. He brings his right arm, hand held in a fist, knuckles forward, down into a protective position in front of his body and raises his left arm high to his left side (figs. 255, 256).

Keypoints: In making the brush-block with his left hand the defender makes contact with the attacker's arm just above the elbow joint. It is important that the defender twist his body to the left as he delivers the whip blow with his right back-fist. Not only does this twist reinforce the blow, but with the shift of weight onto the advanced left leg, it prepares the defender to deliver the roundhouse-kick made from the platform left leg; the left foot must be pivoted outward on the heel to the defender's left side before the kick is made. Note that the defender's right fist protects his groin even from a blow coming from underneath his body.

253

BEGIN HERE

● KEYPOINTS ●

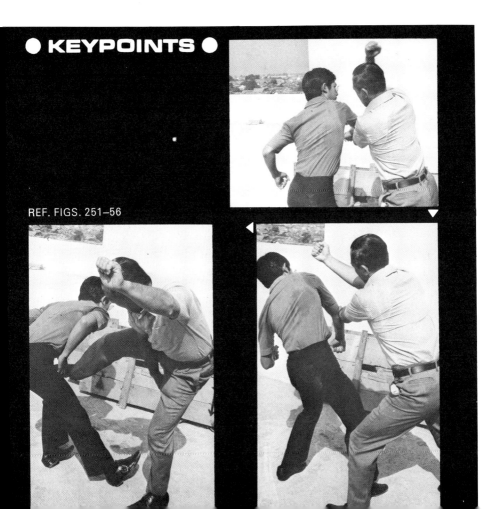

REF. FIGS. 251–56

BEGIN HERE

257

264

265

modern
application

3

266

Situation: This situation and its response may be considered a more severe application of technique in an extension of the preceding situation. An assailant menaces the defender from a left stance, fists clenched, and is about to deliver a roundhouse punch with his right fist to the left side of the defender's head (fig. 257).

ponse: As the attacker steps forward
ɔ his right foot and swings a right
ndhouse punch, the defender brush-
:ks it from the outside with his open
hand; the defender leans well back
is right-rear corner (fig. 258). The
nder keeps his left hand in contact
ι the attacker's right arm just above
elbow, and pushes that arm across his
y to his right and back against the
ιilant's body. At the same time the
nder raises his right arm behind him,
d formed in a fist, knuckles back (fig.
. Quickly the defender twists to his
and lunges forward onto his advanced
leg and delivers a whip blow with
back-fist of his right hand to the right
of the assailant's head, using the base
ckles of the first two fingers as a
:ing surface (figs. 259, 260). The
nder then delivers a roundhouse-kick
ι his right foot to the groin of the
cker, using the upper portion of the
as a striking surface. The defender
gs his right arm into a protective
tion in front of him, fist with knuckles
vard, covering his groin; at the
e time he raises his left arm to a

high position at his left side (figs. 261,
262). After he has delivered the
roundhouse-kick, the defender quickly
steps his right foot to the ground in front
of him and to his right (figs. 263, 264).
As the assailant falls to the ground, the
defender delivers a hammer blow with
the back-fist of his right hand against
the right side of the attacker's head, using
the base knuckles of the first two fingers
as a striking surface (figs. 265, 266).

Keypoints: The keypoints for this
application are the same as those for the
preceding situation and response until the
roundhouse-kick has been delivered.
Thereafter the action is extended. The
defender must ensure that he places his
right foot far enough forward and to his
right to enable him to bring the hammer
blow of his right back-fist onto the
target; with this blow the defender must
also lunge well forward to give it added
effect. Notice that the defender carries
his left arm, hand held in a fist, high
above his head behind him; in this
position the left back-fist is ready to be
used in a whip blow if necessary.

269

▼

270

modern application 4

Situation: An assailant stands in a left stance and moves forward to try to kick the defender in the groin (fig. 267).

Response: The defender blends with the force of the attacker's right forward snap-kick by moving backward into a left ready stance; at the same time the defender strikes down simultaneously with both hands in back-fists against the lower portion of the attacker's kicking leg, using the base knuckles of the first two fingers of each hand as striking surfaces (fig. 268). As the attacker withdraws his kicking leg, the defender quickly shifts his weight forward onto his advanced left leg, pivots on that foot to his left, and delivers a roundhouse-kick with his right foot to the groin of the attacker, using the upper portion of his toes as a striking surface. At the same time the defender brings his right arm into a protective position in front of him, hand held in a fist, knuckles forward, covering his groin; he also raises his left arm, hand held in a fist, knuckles up, to a position high at his left side (figs. 269, 270). As the attacker falls, the defender follows up his advantage by stepping his kicking right foot to the ground, heel first, to his right side. At the same time, he bends and raises his right arm, hand held in a fist, to face level in front of him, and raises his left arm, hand held in a fist, knuckles up, to a high position behind him (fig. 271). The defender quickly delivers a hammer blow with the back-fist of his right hand to the right side of the attacker's head, using the base knuckles of the first two fingers of that hand as a striking surface. He follows up this blow with a whip blow of his left back-fist, also to the right side of the falling attacker's head, using the base knuckles of the first two fingers of that hand as a striking surface (figs. 272, 273).

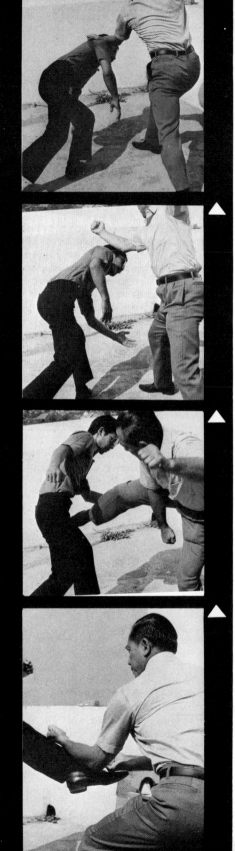

138

● KEYPOINTS ●

Keypoints: The defender moves into the left ready stance by slide-stepping his feet backward (right foot, then left foot He makes the double back-fist blow by bringing his left fist down hard onto the assailant's right mid-shinbone and right fist down hard onto the attacker's right instep. The defender must blend w the withdrawal of the attacker's kicking leg by pivoting to the left on the heel of his left foot to reinforce the delivery of his roundhouse-kick. Notice the protective role played by the defender's right arm at this point. The position of the defender's right kicking foot on the ground after delivery of the roundhouse kick is very important. It must be place far enough to the defender's right side to bring both his blows, the hammer an the whip, within striking distance of the target.

◀REF. FIGS. 268–73

modern application 5

274 ▼

uation: An attacker has seized the defender by the oat, collar, necktie, or lapels with the left hand, and is eatening to punch his face with the right fist (fig. 274).

sponse: The defender raises his left arm, hand held in a , and brings the upper outer surface of his left forearm, r the wrist, down hard against the attacker's left arm m the inside; he twists his upper body slightly to his t to reinforce this striking action (fig. 275). Immediately, defender shifts his weight onto his right leg and raises left leg by bringing the thigh parallel to the ground; he ckles his body forward at the waist, jutting his buttocks kward. At the same time, the defender bends and hdraws his left arm, hand held in a fist, knuckles down, his left side; he also raises his right arm, bringing it, d held in a fist, knuckles up, into a protective position ront of him at face level (fig. 276). The defender then s well forward with his raised left leg to a position ween the assailant's legs. At the same instant, the ender lunges well forward over his advanced left leg and vers a thrust-punch with his left fist to the attacker's , using the base knuckles of the first two fingers as a king surface. The defender simultaneously withdraws right fist to a position alongside his right temple, ckles facing back (fig. 277).

points: The best place for the defender to strike with his arm blow is the biceps of the attacker's left arm. By ing his left thigh parallel to the ground, the defender ses the assailant to anticipate a kicking action; at this nt the attacker may be hesitant to punch with his right for fear he will need his right arm to block the icipated kick. But the kick never comes. The defender ely uses the raised left leg to accelerate his step forward reinforce his left thrust-punch. Study the twisting ons made by the defender. First he twists to his right to ver the forearm block, then he twists back to the front e raises his left leg, and finally, with the thrust-punch is left fist, he twists once more to his right to increase force of that punch.

275 ▼

276 ▼

277

● KEYPOINT ●

REF. FIG. 275

modern application

6

Situation: This emergency situation is identical to the preceding one. But the response is different, and more severe. The attacker has seized the defender by the throat, collar, necktie, or lapels with the left hand, and is threatening to strike his face with the right hand (fig. 278).

Response: The defender strikes his left forearm down hard on top of the biceps of the attacker's left arm from the inside, reinforcing the blow by twisting his upper body to his right. At the same time the defender withdraws his right arm, hand held in a fist, knuckles down, to his right side (figs. 279, 280). Quickly the defender shifts his weight onto his right leg and simultaneously delivers a blow with his right fist and a kick with his left foot. He uses his right fist in thrust-punch fashion to strike the attacker full in the face, using the base knuckles of the first two fingers as a striking surface; this action is reinforced by a withdrawal of his left arm, hand held in a fist, knuckles down, to his left side. At the same time the

281

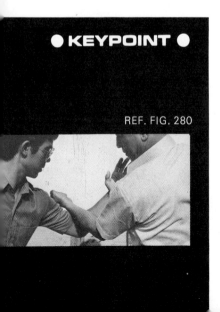

● KEYPOINT ●

REF. FIG. 280

nder delivers a forward snap-kick his left foot into the attacker's groin below, using the instep of that foot striking surface (figs. 281, 282). defender then steps his kicking left down, well forward to a position een the assailant's legs; as he does the defender lunges well forward onto now advanced left leg and delivers a ard thrust-punch with his left fist he chin of the assailant, using the base ckles of the first two fingers as a ing surface. The defender reinforces action by withdrawing his right arm protective position, hand held in a knuckles facing back, alongside his t temple (figs. 283, 284).

Keypoints: The keypoints for this situation and its response are the same as those for the preceding situation up to the point when the defender delivers his forearm blocking action to the attacker's left arm. Thereafter, the difference lies in the fact that in the present situation the defender actually delivers a kick with his left foot and a thrust-punch with his right fist. Care should be taken here not to twist too far to the right or you will destroy the position necessary for making the forward snap-kick. After the kick has been made, however, the lunge step forward with the left foot and the twist of the upper body to the right, made to reinforce the blow, are quite pronounced.

278

279

BEGIN HERE

283

282

290

289

291

292

142

modern
application
7

287 286 285

...ation: An assailant has seized the defender's right wrist ... his left hand and is menacing the defender, who stands ...ng him (fig. 285).

...onse: The defender quickly captures and controls the ...ilant's attacking left arm by flexing his right hand ...ard and driving it up under the assailant's wrist to ...p it in the fork of the hand that lies between thumb ...forefinger; simultaneously the defender raises the ...ilant's attacking arm to shoulder level in front of him ...286). Without pausing, the defender brings the ...cker's captured left arm over in front of his body to ...eft until it is in a low position; keeping his feet in place ...e pivoting on them, the defender twists his body to ...eft to reinforce his action against the assailant's left ...(figs. 287–89). Suddenly the defender jerks the attacker's ...ured left arm to the right and pulls downward along ...long axis of that arm; the assailant's weight is brought ...his rear left leg (figs. 290, 291). The defender then ...vers a low roundhouse-kick with his right foot against ...back of the attacker's left leg just below the calf near ...Achilles' tendon, using the instep as a striking surface ...292). By a combined hook-kick upward and a pull ...is right arm downward on the attacker's captured left ..., the defender sends the attacker sprawling (fig. 293).

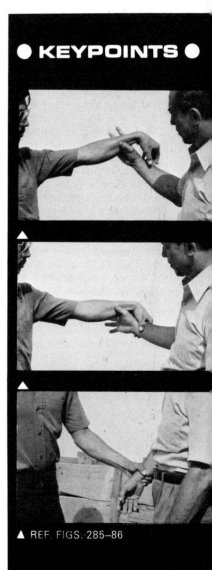

● KEYPOINTS ●

▲ REF. FIGS. 285–86

● KEYPOINTS ●

Keypoints: The defender must seize, move, and control the assailant's left arm. Study the three distinct stages of this action. Note that in the second, or moving, stage the defender is firmly grasping the assailant's wrist and is actually pulling that arm forward and downward as he rotates the arm to bring the elbow up. Any resistance offered by the assailant at this point, such as an attempt to pull back with his captured left arm or to right his posture, will actually aid the defender in forcing the assailant's arm back and across to the defender's right side in the third, or control, stage of this technique. Then the defender's downward-pulling force must result in pinning the assailant onto his left foot. To be able to deliver a low roundhouse-kick in a hooking manner the defender must slide his left foot in cross-step fashion in front of his right leg, bringing the left foot, toes pointing to his left, near the assailant. By a quick shift of weight onto the left leg, the defender uses it as a platform from which to deliver the low roundhouse-kick.

REF. FIGS. 287–89

145

glossary

Unless otherwise indicated, Chinese terms are in the Mandarin dialect.

GENERAL

ch'uan 拳   fist
ch'uan-fa 拳法   artful use of fists
ch'uan-shu 拳術   artful use of fists
ch'uan-tou (Hokkien: kun-tao) 拳頭   "head of the fist"
chung-kuo ch'uan 中國拳   Chinese fist-art
hou 猿   monkey
hsing-i 形意   name of an internal system of sparring tactics
hsiung 熊   bear
hsiung-niu 雄牛   bull
hu 虎   tiger
i 意   will, mind, mental spirit
kung-fu (Cantonese) 功夫   a generic term for exercise
kun-tao, see ch'uan-tou
kuo-shu 國術   national art
lohan 羅漢   *arhat,* or scholar-priest
lung 龍   dragon
nei-chia 內家   internal systems
nei-kung 內功   internal power, inner strength
pai 派   an organization for perpetuating a system of hand-to-hand tactics

glossary

pai-ho 白鶴　white crane
pa-kua 八卦　name of an internal system of sparring tactics
pao 豹　leopard
Shaolin 少林　substantially external systems of sparring and grappling
　　tactics
she 蛇　snake
song-ti-chou 宋太祖　emperor
t'ai-chi ch'uan 太極拳　name of an internal system of sparring tactics
Ta Mo 達摩　Bodhidharma
t'ang-lang 螳螂　praying mantis
tao-chien 套拳　prearranged exercise
wai-chia 外家　external systems
wai-kung 外功　external power, outer strength
wu-kung 武功　martial endeavor
wu-shu 武術　martial art, martial arts
yang 羊　ram
yang 陽　active, positive, "male" principle of the universe
yin 陰　passive, negative, "female" principle of the universe
ying 鷹　eagle

FUNDAMENTALS AND TRAINING

cha 捶　"whip" action of fist
chao-tie 抄踢　low roundhouse-kick
ch'i 氣　vital power
ch'i-kung 氣功　power of ch'i
chi-ma-sze 騎馬式　"horse-riding" or deep crouching stance
fung-shou 撻手　lock-turning action
kai-kung-sze 開弓式　"bow-drawing" or deep archer's stance
kai-tang-sze 開襠式　"chest-opening" or lunge stance
kek 捶　thrust-punch
kua-hu-sze 跨虎式　"tiger" or stalking stance
liang-ke-tie 兩個踢　forward double snap-kick
lien tao-chien 練套拳　solo training
pu-fa 步法　stepping movement
pung 掤　"hammer" action of fist
sien-chi-sze 玄難式　"fighting cock with spurs" or ready stance

sien-fung-tie 旋乞式　whirlwind-kick

sze 式　stance and posture
tao-chien 套拳　prearranged exercise
ten-san-sze 登山式　"mountain-climbing" or exertion stance
tie 踢　forward snap-kick
tu-lie-sze 獨立式　"one-leg" or balancing stance
twee-chee tao-chien 對捌套拳　training with a partner
yeh-sing-sze 夜行式　"walking and searching in the night" or stealth
  stance

WEAPONS

cha 尺　two-tined iron truncheon; also called *titcher*
chang 扚　knife-edge of hand
ch'iang 鎗　straight-bladed spear
chien 劍　straight, double-edged long sword
chiet 掌　open palm
ch'uan 拳　fist
goh 勺　beak-hand
kung-chi 工器　weapons
kung-pang 棍棒　staff
kwan-tao 關刀　long-handled halberd
liang-chet-kwon 兩節棍　two-sectioned stick
piao 鏢　short throwing blade
san-cha 三叙　three-pronged spear, or trident
san-chet-kwon 三節棍　three-sectioned stick
swang-so-tai 雙手帶　short-handled halberd
tao 刀　curved, single-edged long sword
titcher 鐵尺　*see* cha

ABOUT THE AUTHORS   **Tjoa Khek Kiong**, now an Indonesian citizen with the name Leo Budiman Prakarsa, is a master-teacher of Chinese martial arts and also a judoka of senior black belt level, who as a leading instructor in Indonesia has developed national judo champions and has served as Indonesia's national judo coach. He now lives in Jakarta.

Donn F. Draeger, the well-known authority on Asian martial arts and weapons, is an active practitioner of many fighting systems, a far-ranging researcher, and the founder and director for research of the International Martial Culture Research Center in Hawaii. He is also a lecturer at the East-West Center and the University of Hawaii. **Quintin T. G. Chambers**, a licensed instructor of various Japanese martial disciplines, is a staff hoplologist at the International Martial Culture Research Center and the senior editor of the magazine *Martial Arts International*.

The "weathermark" identifies this book as a production of John Weatherhill, Inc., publishers of fine books on Asia and the Pacific. Supervising editor: Suzanne Trumbull. Book design, typography, and layout: Pascal Krieger. The text is set in 9- and 10-point Monotype Times New Roman.